NIGHT
TRAIN
TO
TUXTLA

Camino del Sol

A Chicana and Chicano Literary Series

Series Editor
  Ray Gonzalez

Editorial Committee
  Francisco Alarcón
  Rudolfo Anaya
  Denise Chávez
  Pat Mora

NIGHT TRAIN TO TUXTLA

Juan Felipe Herrera

THE UNIVERSITY OF ARIZONA PRESS | TUCSON & LONDON

Grateful acknowledgment is given to the following magazines and journals in which some of these poems first appeared:

After Aztlán: Latino Writing in the Nineties, American Poetry Review, Argonaut, Best American Poetry—1992, Bloomsbury Review, Boston Review, Conditions—West River Review, Currents Dancing Beneath the River (HBJ), Guadalupe Review, High Plains Review, Lusitania, Mid-American Review, Mirrors Beneath the Earth, Oxygen, New England Review, New England Review Anthology, Río Grande Review, Threepenny Review, Tonantzín, and the *Santa Clara Review.*

"Memoria(s) from an Exile's Notebook of the Future" and "City Paint" were published in a limited edition chapbook, *Memoria(s) from an Exile's Notebook of the Future,* published by the Santa Monica College Press, Lalo Series, 1993.

Library of Congress Cataloging-in-Publication Data

Herrera, Juan Felipe.
    Night train to Tuxtla / Juan Felipe Herrera.
      p.   cm. — (Camino del sol)
    ISBN 0-8165-1459-3 (alk. paper) — ISBN 0-8165-1485-2 (pbk. : alk. paper)
    1. Mexican Americans—Literary collections.   I. Title.
II. Series.
PS3558.E74N54   1994
811'.54—dc20   94-6878
                                        CIP

British Library Cataloguing-in-Publication Data
A catalogue record of this book is available from the British Library.

For Margarita

Contents

Train Notes

I owe my love for writing to my mother, Lucha Quintana, who at any point and in any place would rise from the table and recite poems. Or she would dance in a small circle with her hands up, in gypsy air—in our living room.

Little by little my mother managed to show me the magic of her inner words and worlds. My father, Felipe, loved *cuentos*. He had a bag of stories from the early 1900s—about jumping trains from Chihuahua to El Norte to Cheyenne, Wyoming, about working cattle, the roads, and the earth. Through the years, regardless of the abrupt changes in our lifestyle in *migrante* camps or small towns of the Southwest, my parents always found moments to trade stories and to read from whatever print was available. My mother picked up the newspaper, my father sat back quietly with his old Baptist Bible. Or they would perform in the front yard or *el porche,* with *adivinanzas,* riddles, like the one about el Indio de Acapul and more cuentos like the one about the mountain camp where they paid you in gunny sacks of sweet potato or the one about having to go back to a life on the road, about changing residence because my father had the quixotic belief that moving changed one's body cells and kept the world fresh.

Later, I tested my father's traveling philosophy and found it to be true. Being an only child made our home a simple and consistent theater forum. When I couldn't go anywhere, because we didn't have an automobile for many years or a phone at all, I would simply project myself into that new terrain and imagine myself taking part in its ambience. Or I would quite naturally walk alone in the open fields, small ranches, and mountain ranges and taste the air. In the late afternoons and in the evenings, I would listen to my father's tales. His stories entertained and enlightened me, especially the tale about paying one cent for each word he learned in English. My father's *chistes* were my favorites. "Once there were three men," he would say, "*el calvo, el mocoso y el roñoso*" (the Bald Man, the Runny Nose Man, and the Itching Man). The three aggrieved men were all sitting on the same bench under the scorching sun. None of them wanted to share their private suffering, so they made up ways of covering their individual maladies without risking notice. The bald man, for example, covered his head from the burning rays by slapping his pate in surprise, as if he had just spotted a horse in the distance.

My mother was more dramatic and passionate, and more intent on guiding me through the world of letters; when I was about four years old, she began to teach me how to read in English and Spanish with stories from outdated primers found in Goodwill stores. And she would sing the songs of her childhood in the barrios of Mexico City and El Paso, Texas—melodies from the twenties and thirties. She is also the one who inspired me to take great risks with my art, my thinking, and my life—there are times when I wish I would have been a bit more cautious like my father.

Only now do I realize how deeply these early tellings impressed me. I thank them first, Lucha and Felipe, for their love, their true ways, for their many gifts, and for their awareness of the golden smile that lives inside language, may they rest in peace.

These writings are a quest for a personal deepness, for the expression of a more intimate voice. They are a jaunt to my own beginnings, to places I have traveled in search of myself and in search of terms that bring about communion. They are also sketch pads for writing experiments, for the crossing-over of various "voicings" into new ways of speaking-writing. In some instances, I have come back, full circle, to my own talk, the talk of my parent's house and my *vecinos,* singing Chicano. In other moments, I have slipped, willfully, into other rendezvous.

Previously, I had not taken the time to write on the swashbuckling Chicano sixties, an amorphous, open-ended moment of creative and political gestation. Since I had spent the early seventies writing and performing political pieces ribboned with neat Amerindian utopian flourishes, I wanted to reenter, except this time with a more private palette, and unleash a Munch-Mariachi scream—a techno-urban culture gasp jammed up in the thorax. With Santana, I wanted to take on this challenge;

let the congas and midnight beach waves come into the writing—lie down on a bed of hot dream rice stewed in salsa. Let Santana come with a dark spiraled guitar.

It is difficult to speak of my writing experiments since they are mostly unprocessed and still in motion, still cooking. One of the directions in this collection is to allow flavors and textures to speak louder than words, to let the environment locate the senses; what is taking place, what is real; to play more with color, motion, taste buds, style, and the various contours of place, voice, landscape, and people; to let phrase, dialogue, language shards, storytelling take charge. In some cases to let the tables turn, just a bit.

My original impulse for writing some of the "Santana" pieces comes from knowing and watching the Los Angeles-based Latino comedy troupe, Culture Clash. In a couple of cases I took dialogue-strips from their performance of "A Bowl of Beings" and converted these into titles. I did this as a tribute to the ensemble, to Santana's music, and as a salute to the new wave of Latina and Latino performance-comedy.

In other moments, I let the "train" go to places of fear and trembling. This was one of my tasks in the sections "Night Train to Tuxtla" and "On the Day of the Dead, Mr. Emptiness Sings of Love." At each step of the way through the journey, I checked with myself: How do I feel about what I am saying? How does this piece feel on its own? Can I look at this pain? Where is the ecstasy? How to voice it, write it? I wanted to get in between the image and the projector; to eavesdrop on the past, the present, and the future; to find a mirror ribbon under language itself and float through the greenish underside of stanza, icon, syntax; to bend content against pleasure, history against desire, form against flow—to flow trackless.

Sometimes the texts document neither the day realm nor the night realm but rather the twilight or dawn, as in "The Black Christ of Los Angeles," a poem on the recent Los Angeles riots. Here, I wanted the text to take on the proportions of a video mural more than an acrylic portrait, a drone wave more than a soliloquy. The difficulty was in getting inside the story. I didn't want to stay outside on the safe soapbox of the "writer" or "political-poet." I became aware of my limits in this poem when traveling to Venice, California, on a reading tour with Amiri Baraka in early May 1992—a week after the riots. I hadn't been to Venice since the late sixties when I had lived there; the faces in the audience were ashen, the people's skin was raw from the rubbing of anguished hands and from the steely edges of violence still in the air. I knew then, that as much as I had tried, I still remained distant. Nevertheless, I kept this video mural of the splayed infernos walking on two legs; I kept on.

Other entries reach back into other sections of the book and move foreword into new spaces, at times carrying the *sabor* of the previous tellings. This is the case with some of the pieces in "Night Train to Tuxtla." Having gone to Mexico a number of times and into Central America, Guatemala, and El Salvador during the last three decades, I wanted to include documents from some of those travels; I wanted to create a voice sequence that wove in the faces and hearts from distant yet related regions. I wanted to disassemble the cultural and political border-work and create my own continent, through language and the "seeing" that it offers.

The train is a terrible metal machine turned into a delicate soothsayer swishing on two eternal rivers of silver. Trains are made of dreams and steel; if I could only touch on this elusive and sparkling swiftness in the poems, I would be satisfied. The title poem was initially sketched in 1982 after a train ride from Mexico City to Vera-cruz. More than a decade later, after not having resolved the poem, I returned to Mexico again, this time to San Cristóbal de Las Casas, Chiapas, on a personal jour-ney. When I returned to the States, I rewrote and finished the poem in fifteen minutes. "Zeta" tells of a similar journey south, into Panama. Here, I conjure the lost body of the Chicano artist on the continuous trek into himself; how do we deal with the U.S. military invasion into our body, into the Americas? Also, in this poem, I call up the shadow-figure of Oscar Zeta Acosta, a Chicano poet-lawyer-novelist reportedly lost or murdered in Mexico in 1974.

This has been one of my key concerns as a writer: to unearth the stories about the Chicano and Latin American experience. And yet it is not pure archaeology since language recreates itself, the speakers, and the events. We could even say poetry is an anti-archaeology that subverts history, the writer, and the audience; it is more concerned with an open-ended present and the Möbius strip of reality, per-ception, and the word. "What is?" Every poem loves this question.

My task revolves around a simple reflection: Can I move a little closer to what is taking place, a couple of more centimeters toward intimacy?

I want this collection to be a word dance among familiar friends, figures that have been slipping and sliding on my table and in my house for the last two decades: language dancers, swirled jottings, fast soul-tappings, journal-steppers. I made an effort to stay alert to their ways and styles and yet at every turn and swoop they have outguessed me. In many instances the tellings linger between imagined moments and "factual" occasions. They stretch from narratives into dream journals, from prose poems into street riffs, from accounts into invocations, from Movimiento memoirs to Día de los Muertos meditations in which Mr. Emptiness skates with Lorca-print pajamas, in which the text itself becomes opaque with masks, fresh coffins, and erotic pastels — to international letters written to hammer writers: those who bust walls across the oceans, with breath, defiance, with living — to Berlin.

This is, in a way, my own Southwest shuffle, a zoom-zoom train of travels into myself, my soul languages, and into the communities which I have visited. I never even imagined the journey would require a zoot suit, Chicano rebellious smoke-draped attire pouring through the pages, at times in light festive colors and at others in deeper nocturnal hues and textures. When I found the "suit," I was delighted, I put it on, let it saunter and swagger at times, I jumped a ride, and I let it display its organic snarl. Later, I turned on myself, stripped it off in shreds. I wanted to immerse myself in the pleasures of writing as a Chicano growing up in the fifties, the sixties, the present; I also wanted to leave myself behind at an unknown station, knowing that this would make for deeper voyages.

Too many times our voices have been condemned and negated. As the late novelist and friend, Arturo Islas, said in his last interview published in the *Guadalupe Review*, "We don't even have the privilege of being 'black-listed,' we have been *unlisted*." This reminds me of my blurting out a question in Spanish in an Escondido elementary school in the mid-fifties and being slapped and warned never to speak in Spanish again. I kept this to myself, didn't tell my parents about it; it went deep inside of me. Then little by little I pulled the words out of my mouth, I brought them back out into the open air, the way my parents sang stories out of their experience, the way my mother caressed poems in the air.

∎   ∎   ∎

I want to thank Margarita Luna Robles, my wife, a poet and performance artist in her own right, for her critical insights, feedback, and support. Without her spirit and keen intelligence, I would have faltered. To Ray González, tireless editor and caring poet, for his open enthusiasm and encouragement through the years. Without his invitation, I would not have assembled this volume. To Joanne O'Hare, senior editor at the University of Arizona Press, who gave me an open space on which to lay these poems down. And, to the editors and publishers of small-press books and magazines who have published my work through the years. Special gracias to El Centro Cultural de la Raza of San Diego for publishing my first book, *Rebozos of Love* in 1974, to Ernesto Padilla and Yolanda Luera of Lalo Press for putting out my second, *Exiles of Desire* in 1983, to John Marron of Dragon Cloud Press for the third, *Facegames* in 1987, and to Stephen Kessler of Alcatraz Editions for *Akrílica* in 1989. Without them I would still be looking out the window on "F" Street next to the Sunbeam Bakery in San Diego, California, where I spent my junior high and high school days. I thank Lauro Flores and Rudolfo Anaya for reading through my work, taking notes, writing about it, for their friendship and encouragement. To my uncle Roberto Quintana Martínez who in the forties brought the *pachuco* comedy of Tin Tan to the airwaves in Juárez, Chihuahua; to my uncle Geno who took a number at Fort Bliss, El Paso, for the sake of bringing our family to the United States; to my aunts Aurelia, Teresa, and Alvina, who showed me the survival puzzle: the lot that has been given to Mexican women and how they transform it. To Mrs. Sampson, my third-grade teacher at Lowell Elementary in Logan Heights, San Diego, for stirring my voice toward music; to Mr. Hayden, my sixth-grade teacher at Patrick Henry Elementary in San Francisco, for inviting me to think as an actor; to Mr. Wightman at San Diego High, for introducing me to Descartes and cartoons. And thanks to Tomás Ybarra-Frausto, Fernando Alegría, Ishmael Reed, George Barlow, Marvin Bell, Gerald Stern, and Jorie Graham for lending me their musical ears. Much appreciation to Barbara Firoozye for fine-tuning this manuscript. Finally, to all my *camaradas,* poets, musicians, artists, *teatristas,* community-lovers, who showed me the way: how to speak and write poems in two easy steps called love and spirit. To my friends and teachers who have given of themselves, who have offered me their stories and lives. To my stepchildren, Marlene and Robert Segura, who have traveled with me and have rounded out my soul, and my own children, Joaquín, Almasol, and Joshua, who recognize the tracks; this is for all of them. Gracias.

NIGHT
TRAIN
TO
TUXTLA

Ya repican las campanas,
ya comienza a andar el tren
le pregunto a míster Hill
que si vamos pa' Luisiana.
"El Contrabando de El Paso,"
Corrido Chicano

The train plunges on through the pitch-black night
I never knew I liked the night pitch-black
Sparks fly from the engine
I didn't know I loved the sparks . . .
"Things I Didn't Know I Loved,"
Nazim Hikmet

LISTENING
TO
SANTANA

Zoot Suit on a Bed of Spanish Rice

When one of us dies you can tell.

A swarm of children in black. Notice how El Greco paints us into the barrio scene. The men are short, then elongated, going up into the turbulent skies, stilled by a crazy figure inside and outside: a charcoal Madonna with the face of Martha Graham, except more oval and with a seductive mouth. Their bent, tiny heads glimmer. For a second or two. A couple of shots are heard. Four shots—a military salute for the wrap in the casket—the way my uncle Geno went down into the ground in '57.

Behind tombstones.

Hide and go seek with Chente, my cousin. Both of us have buck teeth and we laugh like girls. Mama is the only one crying, she leans down into the soft earth and pulls up the bluish pit in her soul. When I cry—silence. Sometimes it comes in little beeps. Gets jammed somewhere on my upper back, near the neck. Useless, most of the time. A few years ago I made peace with another uncle, Roberto Q. Five carnations. We never talked. Made candy, pink-striped bars wrapped in cellophane in his basement. Got busy, later—a poet with four kids. Riding around Stanford in a '54 yellow Ford pickup. Wore bell-bottoms and aced the classes. Except Collier's statistics; you can always catch a Chicano flunking statistics. This was my first folly at Stanford. The second was disappearing for an entire summer in Mexico to live the life of Cagney in Cuernavaca and Brando in Acapulco. At 5:00 a.m., hang out the window of the Hotel Regency Presidente—eight floors up. Gaze over the bay, baby, inhale the green air, love the sweetness from the sky. Alcohol from my ledge and gasoline from speedboats and the helicopters, the ones that take you up in a nylon kite for four hundred pesos. Come down and drink gin gimlets in the pools. Make love to a secretary from Tegucigalpa. An accident. That's what I said when I got back.

When my mother died my shirt tightened. Cried for six years. Shaved my mustache. Shaved my head. Wanted to cut myself down to size. Strip the skin off. Because I couldn't feel it. Think of ukuleles, I told myself. Oblong brown chocolate ones with good strings. Or Hawaiian shirts at the National Dollar store in San Diego where we used to go shopping in the fifties; Jergens, Three Roses pomade, khakis for fifth grade. Airplane glue in a sock hanging out with Raymond and Arnold and Miguel. Every ghost boy I know. They show up with my uncles now—smoke rings on my bruised face.

The therapist says, Just a couple of visits. I show my teeth. Is it a peppermint flavor inside my lips? Or is it fire?

Sport a flat top now. Think of the days—original flat top days and Roman Meal bread, soft speckled stuff the doctors prescribed for my mother. My father was alive then too. Makes me laugh when he does his special imitation of a gun going off. Does this the same way he makes dove sounds. Pulls his lower lip down with his thumb and forefinger. Then he breathes backwards.

Cook at least three things, learn, he said.

Rice, the long red pointed kind stewed with burnt tomatoes. Enchiladas, the apartment kind, folded with onions and Kraft cheese. They can be served anywhere to anyone. Char the salsa too, on an iron grill. Mash the green-black pulp inside a stone bowl. The one that rocks on three legs.

Let Yourself Be Sidetracked by Your Güiro

Let yourself be sidetracked by your güiro
let yourself be free . . .

Alurista, 1971

Never took anyone's advice.

Just put on my white plastic thongs, my muslin bell-bottoms and slammed the road. Up Santa Monica Boulevard. Down Venice Beach. Sunset Strip if I had the right jacket—an ex-Sidney Poitier thing was best.

Maybe it was the acid, the Purple Haze tabs. Maybe it was the memory of my old mother listening to Bobby Vinton as she prayed to la Virgen, walked over to her window on Mission Street. Peered at the Thor Hotel junkies, hunched and wise, tossing beers at each other. You catch them on the escape ladders, rolling up sleeves. Shoot up, in style. Or maybe it was my dead father who I would never talk about. Fever. This fever of a mad brown child. And it was the incense. Patchouli and madras and sandalwood. Frankincense and vanilla. Sometimes carnation flower oil is best, especially after you smooth your Gibson acoustic—finish it off with a geranium oil rub.

Easy, homeboy.

This was the breeze I carried after I broke up with a Jewish Russian Chicana named Romero. Fast and fragrant. I was never so pure. So light. She had decided to make it with other women and Angelo, an olive-skinned teen from East Los going to Santa Monica High. The day before we had made a new batch of tahini enchiladas and garbanzo *mole*. One of our new Cinco de Mayo specialties.

After the breakup, every morning: jump sturdy and dream through my forty-five-minute yoga routine. Picked it up from Judith Drake, a fifty-year-old Marilyn Monroe who will hypnotize you with her sienna braid and her cosmic muscularity, not to mention her spinal juice—an energy snake syrup she said we all swish inside and all that we have to do is shout out the names of our ancestors. Think benevolence and walk as if you are shuffling tiny pomegranate bubbles of champagne effervescence. You could find me beneath a eucalyptus in the backyard. Actually, the tree was part of a tidy landscape groomed by the Irish geologist that lived upstairs. Helped him plant cilantro until the stuff mutated into a ferocious weed. Splayed heads that jump and weave around the compost pile.

Sweet as clover, I told the geologist, when Romero and I moved in.

When we moved in it was another matter. Had just arrived from Mexico. A deep, deep journey. Didn't want to shake it out of my system. Kept it moving inside— rented a formal family house on South Bentley Street in Santa Monica.

Meditate and listen to the voices, I said to myself. Keep the sounds alive. Write. Wasn't in the habit of writing every day or every other day—this came later. An orangutan writer, that was me. Hang in the lofty rooms. Or take long intense walks on my pointed sandals that I brought back from Oaxaca. Cruise up the streets. Write on yellow pads. Cross the avenues into nowhere. Keep all the stuff in mind, don't let it get you—what came down in Mexico. Crack the page, homeboy, take a hard look: the drive that ended up in an explosion of steel confetti, the marihuana stack in front of the Huichol shaman who laughed about it, said it wasn't what you smoked, the Indian banana truck that rammed into our Chevy pickup, the forged traveler's checks, the soapy road from San Cristóbal de las Casas to Tuxtla Gutiérrez. We're gonna hit the big Chicano number, I told my friends.

I made it back to the homeland, drained. Yellowish, broken. Beaten by three or four thousand miles of mosquitoes, Delicado and *grifa* smokes. Indian cane juice. Indian drills into the darkness. Into delicate jungle rivers infested with malaria. Didn't know how to talk about it. Kept my mouth shut.

Carry the music inside. Night driver beaner music . . .

Listen: a Miles Davis, Coltrane trenchcoat, *huipil, peyote* diesel overcoat, Ferris wheel, bundled mothers in concrete neon profiles, and screaming mothers, and dazzled motherless children, tiny, powdered, puffed hands caressing a tin cup with a frothy human organ pumping saliva—selling or saying something to me. Bounce into the caves, into the tents, gas stations and carnivals. When you get back, homeboy, L.A. will be dressed in flames. East Los—a Spanish colonial garden of bullets and torn hair. Rubén Salazar will be blown away by the L.A. County sheriffs, tapped on the shoulder with a canister of gas as he quietly drinks a cooler at the Silver Dollar. The rest of the throng, the brown bronze ground force will march and demonstrate as usual— to the tune of a Santana piece, maybe "Jingo." Maybe "I Got a Black Magic Woman." Blown.

Blast and beaten to the skull, homey, for rapping and congregating against the Nam war. You will come back to this. Back in Santa Monica.

Just walk ahead, big John, I say.

Into the haze of human shapes, into the mumbling root trunks of the acid trees. Jump sturdy at six, again. Eat that macrobiotic breakfast, a half glass of water and a rice cake brushed with tahini. Remember to tie a large jar of diluted apple juice around the funny belt. My turquoise belt from Veracruz. Snatch a hand of almonds, into a small plastic sandwich bag. Feed the blue jay at the park. Watch him. Lift the big brown ridged seed, Johnny Blue Jay. Scratch this dirt.

A year later. The last time.

I step out from the Bentley house. Romero is in the living room drinking something, looking sideways at me. We have gone through a lot together. Our brains are still spinning and our hands and flesh are still pasty from all our rendezvous. She can't stop and I can't stop. We have albums and Aztec serapes on the wall. One of them has a Buddha-like figure that looks like it's giving birth to another god or goddess. A red scroll of words to the left of the face. Word glyphs in dyed wool.

Romero is into something new now.

Flying up the street—that's me, this guy with the guitar case in one hand and a multi-colored jute bag of seersucker shirts and paper pads in the other. Up the fat avenue with a continuous blare in the head.

How to Do the Merengue in the End Zone

for Culture Clash and Carlos Santana

I am on fire and there is a glassy coolness inside—a black light comes all the way down. My steps are measured and my body is gone.

First time that I heard Santana was on Market Street. The Fillmore West by Van Ness had just opened. He called his band the Carlos Santana Blues Band in those days. There wasn't much to it. You sat back in the hazy circle, exchanging Lucky Strikes and Thai sticks; you smoke, work with your eyes, keep them going as long as you can.

People on stage looked wavy with bluish heads from the spotlights. Sometimes they were reddish too. At the Avalon Ballroom they had sofas, in case you needed to use the microscope in your head. On the way back, take the Muni—people so loaded that one night this man sitting behind me wearing a black body jacket barfed on my back. A heavy splash with a Red Mountain wine and a pastrami-Quaalude blend.

Do the merengue in the end zone.

That's all you can do. This was the Fillmore maxim: Sway, throw your head back, baby, move your hips, keep yourself in a jive beat to avoid the shit coming at you.

Chop the acid and tunnel your way through the underground channels beneath the piers at midnight. The log supports turn into frothy nails and Kandinsky toothpicks. If you drop your merengue, you end up staring at naked breasts on wood and concentric circles beaming out of your hands, which are fists now; dangling ahead of you, taking you to the other side of the tangled canvas, the glowing hairs of the dock lights. Had to keep moving. Even if I was standing still. Santana provided the grease, felt good when he came out with his first mix.

He was a *vato* from Tijuana—
this is called the Tijuana maxim.

You had to be from T.J. to reproduce that kind of sound. From la Colonia del Rubí, Nápoles, Kilómetro 24, Coahuila—from the busted fandango huts near the electric box saloons with swiveling chairs, bucket seat views, kamikazes with pineapple syrup, and an old man in his sixties, maybe late fifties, serving trays of Coronas or Superiores, trading notes on the dog races with the forty-year-old sex worker. Do the hully gully on the table of secondary-school teachers.

The twisted guitar was regular business.

On Saturday, in the afternoons, there is a pause; time to hit the bullring plaza, rub with the throng of erudite Ladino businessmen, whistling Burt Bacharach and shouting for the cut-off ears and tail of the solid bulls—bulls with the cherubic face of Goya. The bull stomach churns up and shoots black oyster juice from the sex organ, comes down, into a magnetic pile, down to the feet of the ballerina-man dressed in his Spanish lace tights, holding up the thin sword—a psychological puzzle of puberty, death and Renaissance manners. From the outer rings, the picture is clear: the Annunciation of the Monitor God, the split hermaphrodite beast of American doom and Indian capitalism, playing out our sacred drama, an Andalusian–New York grave, the one Lorca gave us, brushed up here and there with a *banderilla,* a meat lance the width of three barbecue skewers. The faces go tight, dark and yellow-brown, the braids are brushed back, the trumpets blare and burn from the rafters.

This was the beginning of the Santana sound. This is where the guitar strings are coiled and the hand is set to hit the lead riffs for the band of spotted maracas and a fleet of ragged school buses under a cloud shifting into the shape of a sugary skull.

Uncle Ferni used to take bring me here. The two of us—see Davie Moore and El Ratón Macías punch each other out at night, when the bullring was converted into a man ring.

Or I would go with my mother and my aunt Lela during the day, and we would walk around looking for healers and quacks to sew up the open wounds from years of being Mexican—the tick in the esophagus that was going to explode into a tumor, the continuous bloodletting from the vagina, the boy penis that was inflated and green.

Afterward: a *café con leche*, a stack of rolled *tacos de tripas de leche, de cabeza, de chuleta, de sesos*—guts, head meat, chops and brains—everything is synonymous. This is called the Mexican maxim.

In Mexico any sound will replicate any other sound. A baby crying sounds like an acetylene torch carving through a tourist fender, at times straightening it; the cough of the thirteen-year-old Americana girl sounds like incisions into the belly by the surgeon in the abortion garage; the old man telling you the jawbone-güiro will forecast your future sounds more like the tilting ten-gallon hat of a navy jock going for a Chinese musician's jugular, a Chino from Mexicali, a few miles east.

Some people look away, toward the cornerman with a donkey painted like a zebra. Self-portraits, save them. But, all you have to do is move. Any part of the body will do.

When Santana's first album came out I was strolling Grant Street in North Beach, up by Green Street, a few blocks north of Café Trieste. Ran into a poster shop. Nowadays it's a Vietnamese hardware store or is it Jewish? I was leafing through as always, looking for a good blues piece, maybe Bobby Blue Bland whom I had seen at the Fillmore with Country Joe and the Fish. Maybe Janis or Jimi. Threw my head back by impulse and noticed the Jim Morrison photo on the ceiling. Black light came down to me, pouring blue milk on my shirt and parts of my pants, even my shoe laces were wet. I was sparkling like one of those Day-Glo saints that I had seen at my aunt Lela's place. Floating. The albums came up, first it was the Buffalo Springfield, then a used one by José Feliciano, he was still wearing a formal Arrow shirt and a tie, then something else fell through, the Santana album with the lion head, the white lion with the mane full of ashes, and the ashes fell on a tribe of other faces—above the left gold eye, a silent priestess with the kiss of a jaguar mouth.

Aztec Roses

*for all Centro Cultural workers throughout
the Southwest*

After
Che Guevara was riddled with shrapnel in the pure oxygen of Bolivia with the beard of
Christ and the melancholy face
of an Argentinean baker.

It was after Janis.
After Joplin went down with her Rajput see-through saffron veils, with Kerouac's Roman
candles stuck inside her left arm. Many nights dipped in
rouge velvet
wall-papered rooms with fancy mirrors,
many night-wire sounds after Santana.

(Last time
I saw Santana
was at the Fillmore West on Market Street in the City. Joplin too. Upstage—a bottle
of Southern Comfort in one hand, the other made into a fist. Jabs in small circles—
Chicana power signs, almost.)

After. After.
Che and Janis. Carlos. Aztec roses on my walls.
Varrio gardens. Venice, East Los, *La Logan.*

By February of 1973, I had just moved to Southern Califas again. Decided to make it at the Centro Cultural de la Raza, a feisty *clika* of Chicanos gone Indian. Muralists, poets, long-haired Spanish rice experts, silk screeners of the new Aztlán nation. I was tired of academia based on amphetamines.

Go south, baby.
Big San Diego, I said.

Got in my '53 straight-eight white bondo Buick with a steering wheel the size of a Pancho Villa hat. Never made it. The *volío* blew a few miles out of L.A., three inches from Carson City. Barely wheeled it into a 76 station. Called up Gloria Flowers who went by the code name, El Indio Feo. A UCLA art major I was tight with.

She drove up in her blue and white souped-up Dodge Challenger. Her dad, José, kept all his kids in *firme carruchas.* He was one of the early *mecánicos* and inventors of the Low Rider in Tijuana, back in the forties.

Sold the white weasel for twelve *bolas* and slid into the front seat of Gloria's stock car. Alurista's pad in San Diego, destination one. This is how I applied the music.

Started working for the Centro, an occupied water tank on the edge of Balboa Park right across from the navy hospital. Pushed plywood for the new office, sucked Kodak developer in the closet-sized darkroom working on negatives I had been carrying around from my Indio journeys. Did odd Chicano jobs.

In charge of the cafeteria, for example.

For "Culture Night," wanted things to taste right. Go to Tijuana, buy five hundred *tortas,* two hundred and fifty *de lomo,* the other half de *hamón,* stash them in the *kawela,* then head back in time for the community dinner, feed the people; this was the plan of operation.

Things didn't pop as expected.

On the way back from Tortas el Turco, the main torta joint on la Calle Constitución, a block over from la Calle Revolución, three blocks over from el Mercado Hidalgo where they serve the best *pata de mula* in a Styrofoam cup for hangovers, sexual prowess, and accounting abilities, at the border line, by the five-gallon blue trash can where they dump your mangos, I got busted good for transporting illegal food into the United States. Call this the archetypical Chicano surprise party.

But I had a *movida.*

My Centro partner, Mancillas, whose dad worked an *abarrotes* store in San Ysidro, packed the other two hundred and fifty in his tiny powder blue Volkswagen beetle. But, the mess still followed me. By the time "Culture Night" opened, a few days later, the tortas nearly killed the eighty people who bought the tickets. Forgot about timing.

Bad year for the Centro.
Learning the ropes.
Year later, I was nominated director.

$50.00 per month.
Eating baked brown rice dough balls with organic raisins.

Project one:
The city was up in arms against us because one of the guys, Tupac, published a piece on Indian sovereignty in our tortilla-colored newsletter, *La Mazorca*.

> *San Diego Tribune* headline:
> Indian Rebels Threaten Takeover

At the other end: Aranda, one of the Indian-Chicano beaners, was painting a mural on the inside walls with machine men, open-clawed eagles, Huichol deer, and UFW pyramids and a giant carved fist, a red board flesh rocket coming at you a few feet from the entrance. On the outside, Cosmos Ochoa had just finished a twenty-foot *calavera*, pointing straight at the navy hospital windows across the street. He told me this was based on a Che Guevara guerrilla technique. A typical beaner strategy at getting back at one of our long-standing San Diego enemies. Señora Herminña, one of the elders, made sure we got ready for these onslaughts. She was in charge of the ritual stuff, like breaking pottery on New Year's, fasting, knowing the words, doing the round dance.

The only time I stayed clear of the Centro was when Chuparrosa, another Chicano gone Indian (said he had *familia* in Cochimí pueblo in Baja) hit me with three peyote buds.

Just told the Centro office that I was on business for the rest of the day. Fled into the park chanting some of my poems for protection.

Ipal Nemowani
Ipal Nemowani
Ipal Nemowani

A few hours later I was talking to the blue jays.

Brush people appeared. Huddled inside trees. Could only see their shady legs. Were they hiding? Waiting? I couldn't tell. I was walking by the freeway and a car veered off and stopped a few feet ahead. Heard someone get out but I didn't want to look. Made a motion with my wooden staff, like señora Hermiña said, three circles to the right, then jerked my arm as if pushing against a slab door. Kept on, looked back. No one. Began to run.

Light stems, airy, swishing, floating. Wasn't even breathing. The cars, palm trees and the tiny picnic tables spread with thermos and frankfurters, bright crimsons and sharp whites of the volleyball players zoomed by my *manta* pants, under my *huaraches*. They were ahead of me. I could jump six, seven feet. Leap up into rubbery trees, leap a hundred miles to the silent ground.

Down a straw gully in the park.

There is something moving. About one o'clock in the afternoon. Thick air, leaf streams. Turned to my left—something wavy between me and the short hill ahead, a curtain of hot breath pouring over the dry grasses. Something jittery and almost hissing a few yards ahead, except I couldn't see it. An eye of wind opened up, a pair of hands, cupped, unfolding their fingers, inside the heat strings. Turn back, a voice inside me said, retrace your steps, head back to the Centro. I shot down a valley on the back side of the Museum of Man, then something came at my back. Turned and saw a little boy jogging a few yards behind me. I felt he was playing with me. Kept on. Laughing through the running game. He was wearing a blue shirt, his arms dark like mine, his hair swinging over his forehead. Couldn't get a glimpse of his face; he was looking down, barefoot, wearing old greenish pants. Could hear his fast skipping steps. Turned again, but no one was there, nothing, just high starry palms mixing into the shafts of sunlight, the soft earth trail shadowed by the foliage of the hills.

Sitting now. Cross-legged.
Thinking of the running boy.

Sitting behind the Centro, on a bare mound of dirt, maybe two hundred yards from the building. Smooth the ground with my left hand. A dove flies up. Where did it come from? How could it fly up from the dirt under my hand? The wings made a fluttering sound, loud, then soft feather music.

Words.

Maybe I sharpened myself into a tiny eucalyptus sleeve or acorn. The flower beds during the morning; they came back to me. I could see their nature spirits. Standing at the highest point of the petals. Arms going up, a tiny dance inside. Faceless, without the kind of features or body flutter that we recognize. They stand there, without names, waving up, in the water winds.

Milagros & Ancient Angels

At an early age my mother warned me, You have a star on your forehead, then she pointed at the reddish patch near the inside of my left knee.

This is what saves me. You just don't know how many times I've been saved. Saved from the emptiness sweltering all around us.

Solórzano, a buddy from East Los, sensed it.

He said he wanted to get away from it—ended up as a receptionist in the emergency room at General Hospital. Reading *Popular Mechanics* and looking at blood spurt from matted heads saved me, he says, twisting the pages of the magazine with speaker wiring and lumber on the cover.

Fell into a twenty-foot well in Mexico.

This was 1961, in Atizapán de Zaragoza, a village that specialized in haircuts, tortillas flattened with a dog head-shaped stone and *pulque.* A shaft of wind across the back of my legs pushed me forward to the other side by the pigpen. The smooth-complexioned animals were my favorites; they never let me trick them into eating raw bulbous jalapeños even when I mixed the seeds with corn slush.

Milagros are sudden.

In '70,

walked into South Tepic, Mexico, with Mendoza and Mancillas. A Huichol Indian asked us, Why are you late? I've been waiting for you for a while, he said. How could he know? Three crazy Chicanos from Venice and East Los. No way, I jived. Then he pointed up to the sky as he sat cross-legged on the outskirts of the city, pasting pink yarn on a slab of plywood. Because Tauyepá, Father Sun, told me, he whispered.

Four years later: jammed down a dusty road on the way to Guatemala City; a small troop of soldiers stopped the bus in the middle of the jungle. Pulled me out. The driver jumped in, said, Leave 'im alone.

Made it back again—to the U.S. of A.

Began to drink more carrot juice.

Drank so much I turned into a copper-shoe version of Wayne Newton. My hands were orange peanut shells. A tapioca fondue, a mango Maharishi phenomenon. Turned mango so bad one of my anthro profs, an Australian aborigine scholar at UCLA, called me down from the auditorium in Haines Hall.

You better see a doctor, he stammered from his armchair. Things couldn't be better, I told him: tonight I got tickets to Sonny and Terry at the Ash Grove. Things are going all right. Next week, Richie Havens and Taj Mahal.

Milagros are hard to talk about—you can't clock them or pin them down.

My mother told me stories of men who kicked their wives and then on the following Sunday hobbled on their knees to the Zócalo in Mexico City, all the way to the altar of the church. When I got there years later, I stood on the bloody granite and concrete square.

The cathedral sank to one side.

A young girl played her harmonica with a sudden gentleness. The breathy sweetness mixed with the clouds and the violet striped shawls and the leather of the tourists. An old man in brown jeans, with long sideburns and a thick back, dragged himself into that blackness, below the steeple, into that broken viola of fright and silvery rays, silvery with reddish squares and octagons of stained window faces and on the long varnished counters, a head of a dead saint, bony hands and fingers in a vinegar jar—next to the confessional. Marble slime on the pillars and torso statues. The man said he wanted to go down into the abyss where one of the saints was buried—for all of us to see. He pinned a gold leaf metal heart on the flannel mantle of St. Judas. This was the necessary cargo.

Now they have another church close by where you can toss your milagros on a conveyer belt. This one doesn't smell of bloody pillows and frenzy, the quiet kind, the kind that gets the job done.

Ritual and pneumonia are the key ingredients.

When you break away you will begin to look at yourself in a tender and evil way. This is the starting point of the milagro.

My mother charged me with the care of an ancient angel figure. I am forbidden to mention the name. She told me this after I sliced seven inches into my knee. A safety pin did it while I was sleeping. Good that it happened in the dark. Just wetness on my right hand and my legs. The same knee with the red patch—the one my mother said a friend of hers had read when I was a baby. The gypsy turned to my mother and said things. All I can tell you is this: milagros have to do with a system of star shapes on the body. If you trace the shapes, they will lead you to the miracles. Solórzano didn't know this.

This tiny formula saves me from burning—the fire that consumes me, the fire across the world. And I have seen the fire starters, the men in beige, green, and blue with their pointed faces and flint noses, swiveling their eyes through fences, from undercover vans.

M.O.C.O.S.
(Mexicans or Chicanos or Something)

for Al Robles,
a charter member of the house,
RIP
and La Kathy Ledesma,
still going
strong

I could never figure it out.

What was it? This funny cilantro-shaped fender popping out my chest. Feels like when you swallow a hard-ribbed tortilla chip and it jams in your throat. So you flex your throat muscles. Push it down like a boa, because you are starved. You slide the flared brown tin, way down, but instead of smoothing, the pain sharpens, the chip inflates, jams up again, around the thoracic area, creates its own habitat, lives there a bit, turns into a reddish chrome plate piece.

Then, you are in the Mexican Badlands—
the Chicano-Faustian shit hole, the Kafkian one-room apartment where there is a Catholic bag of crazy apple skulls ready to come flying at your cockroach-armoured back skin. What do I call myself here?

Wittgenstein couldn't even figure out what he was feeling when he tightened his fingers and folded his palm into a fist. Was it temperature? he asked. Position? Centrality? Or was it clarity? Was it Mayan? Was it Eastern clouds with serpentine illumination? What?

In the autumn of '67, the best I could do was jaunt to Beverly Hills whenever possible, run into Saks Fifth Avenue, treat myself to an Italian long-sleeved shirt. No one expects this. None of my revolutionary friends would ever imagine me going up to the second floor, perishing in the men's section. This has always been my weak side,

I admit it. Fine Italian shirts with viridian coloration. French sweaters with an oval neck design—thick weaves in ultramarine. For pants: cherry red extra-thick corduroy and on occasion, pinstripe cinnamon brown, stove pipes—I got this from the Rolling Stones, Brian Jones always wore them.

One time I switched my style and wore a see-through purple shirt that my *novia,* Carol, made from women's maternity fabric. My pants were purple too.

Was in a groove in the autumn of '67.

The only thing that caught me by surprise was Carlos Chávez, a Movimiento buddy stabbed in Venice beach—got in a bad brawl with some beach dopers. Cut bad grass with too much sugar. Came back to our pad, five minutes from the piers, pushing into his distorted stomach, tucking his *tripas* back in.

Late night steak *sanwishes* washed down with sangría. A favorite treat at La Casa Naka, our Chicano pad in Venice. The sangría Hector León made was best, especially if he was in one of his furious redemption moods. Hector had a holy streak. He either was stoned on Hieronymus Bosch or Jesus Christ. But, you could always count on Hector to give you the right red feeling for the rest of the day. Hector missed his father. Always talked about him, cried sometimes, said he never met him; his mother had raised him alone in the City of Commerce, an industrial plutonium pit in the middle of Los Angeles. Hector carried a tiny silver chain around his neck, with a locket where he kept a miniature photo of his dad. I don't think he ever saw or heard from him in all of his seventeen years. It drove Hector to a higher level, I think. We would go up to his pad on Wilshire, smoke up and follow Bosch into the *mole*-draped woods, creep into the shattered eggshell beings that lived there, broken and one eyed. When he made sangría in our kitchen, slamming cut oranges and grapes into a wine-filled tin bucket he'd let his mouth hang open, he would hunch up, mumble words out, like

pura piña,
    tevoyacurar,
        somos Mazatecas
            —la liberación is in your mouth, carnal.

Eyes stretched back.

Carlos got stabbed the same night when I had wolfed an extra-large bag of raw walnuts. Ate so many nuts I had to walk five miles to ease the stone-pain in my rib cage area. Walked all the way to Malibu. On the way back, I found out about Carlos and then about another *carnal,* a Jewish vato named Stein. Stein's favorite saying was "If you are not on the bus, you're off the bus." His face was washed white, his eyes in a spin. Told me there was a guy OD'd in his tub. Said he tried the cold water thing but it didn't work on the bluish body. He knew this guy, Stein said, he was a member of the Life Force student collective in Santa Monica. I had visited Life Force a few times after I had broken up with my wife who was also Jewish. She had moved out of Venice and joined them for a semester. They were into doorless bathrooms, swiveling bedmates, carrot juice, tahini-banana sanwishes, refrigerator billboards detailing chores and holding intense critique sessions on God, jealousy, fear of the body, and political action. Usually they held these raps in yoga-lotus-sitting postures under large canopies of webbed batik sheets in the living room, candles and fava beans in small plates on the carpeted floors.

I recognized the temperature,
the positions of the internal helix,
the clarity of ocean alphabets, the distance, and the proximity of the cloud people.

I was a Mexican the same way Bosch was Mexican. I was Mexican or Chicano the same way Wittgenstein was Mexican or Chicano. It was all in his gesture, his search for the feeling when he pressed his skin against his skin. What was it he asked, what was it?

I had left home many years ago. Was living now in a wild-city rampage with a cool bass riff underneath. All I had left were the fast colors, flaring, and scarin', flying. On my Kawasaki, in my '59 flared Mercury without side windows and an oval steering wheel melted down from going too deep into Arizona, on a love-chase, after Margarita del Toboso who was holed up in a village a few miles from Prescott, a tiny thirteen-family town on the opposite slope of the Tonto Forest. I found her two decades later, but she was in San José.

All I had were just a few numbers to play with, a few oblong packs of edgy phrases, and a burning portion of a tiny bridge, the one I reached when I jump-started the Kawasaki. An American bridge. I think all of us wanted to get across this busted bridge-line. Behind us, America, in front of us America. Maybe, the greater questions had to do with the bridge itself. What was it made of? How many could it hold. Why was it burning so fast—

red, yellow, red, red.

Rolling to Taos on an Aztec Mustang

for Florencio Guerrero Yescas,
in memory

17 miles
south of San Diego, in Tijuana
next the Hipódromo.

Been here before,
betting on hungry dogs
with tiny T-shirts

racing after a handkerchief
dipped in hot salsa.

Talking to the Mexican
consulate man. (Since I got the *jale*
at the Centro Cultural in San Diego,
I bring *la gente* over
from México—on an artist visa).

Esplendor Azteca, I tell
the consulate man. Five
native dancers from Mexico City,

hardwood *tambores,*
copal incense in ancient burners
two thousand green beads, yarn,

and the taste of petroleum, flavor
of licorice from growing up Mexicano,

from stalling between
oil refineries, fortune-telling parakeets
and candy makers.

The troupe:
Florencio, *el maestro,*
with the cherubic face of Pedro Infante
(he's the one that taught Amalia Hernández
at Bellas Artes in Mexico City)
makes the *danzante* costumes
with anything that you can find,

a Virgen de Guadalupe
etched with needles or with a quarter
on a round slice of metal,
a 7-Up can, for example.

Piolín, from varrio Tacubaya
a rib cage shaped like New York,
puckers his mouth when he talks,
says he's never going back
to La Capital.

Conejo, short, dark
with the face of George Harrison, ex-Beatle.

When Conejo wants
to leave he says,

"Let's gotas,"
when things are getting difficult,
"La hacemos, la hacemos."

Lázaro—he's the one who listens
to Florencio's stories about *la danza,*
how to care for the fire, how to make
friendship with the flame, so it won't burn you—;
he keeps these stories, in his young silence
nourishes them with his own design.

Chepe-chepe,
short for José and Pepe
doesn't look the part.

His hair is short, curly—then
he's got a goofy laugh, shuffles instead
of walking the line.

"Me voy a casar en los estados,"
he says, rubbing his *penacho.*

And Cerillo, from Tacubaya too—
a tall, thin boy, a matchstick
with big wet eyes. He's the drummer,
stoic, sad—precise.

When we got to San Diego
from Tijuas, I asked Alurista and Irene
if Esplendor could stay with us.

(I had a room upstairs overlooking
a eucalyptus on Grove Street. In the closet

one pair of pants,
one pair of string huaraches,
a couple of *camisas,* a white cotton,
a see-through green Hindu shirt,
and a guitar that I borrowed from the Centro.

Grove Street is famous. This is
where San Diego Raza attempted
to build a Marxist Indian commune
in early '71; ask Viviana Zermeño,

or Alurista's old roommate, Jorge
"Krishna" Gonzales.)

So, we tied a red flannel strip
on our foreheads before we left
for the Floricanto II festival
in Austin, Texas—our first stop.

We figured the red strip
would identify us among thousands
of poets, dancers, and *artistas.*

When we passed El Paso
in Mario Aguilar's white Mustang,
I thought of my mother, Lucha,
who grew up in el Segundo Varrio.

I thought of la *calle* Kansas,
la Stanton,
Paisano Drive,
la Overland,
la Segunda,
la Tercera,
la Poplar—

the streets were fragments
of an incomplete story I carried.
Part of me still lived there, an unknown
infant in half-shapes, wondering
for the other lost half.

I wanted to stop, walk into myself again,
but we didn't have time.

Conejo (who didn't know
how to drive)
popped a *llanta*
thirty meters from Sonora, Texas,
a small town with one gas station
and two fast curves.

The Mustang was the kitchen:
while Mario drove, Piolín
cut green tuna cans and made
cracker tacos.

On the road, cracker tacos
are smart. Smarter than eggplant
or spaghetti.

We passed Johnson City
talked about LBJ as gateposts
and nettles washed by the fenders.
Vietnam was still in the air.
The only thing that saved me
from the draft was a bad case of hepatitis,
otherwise I would have gone
on the road,

like Patadas,
a carnal, still hiding out in Santa Monica—
Colby Street, in a garage with tree-stump end tables,
a Bartlett pear tree—this was 1969.

Lázaro asked me about Floricanto.
I told him,

"These are our songs,
this is how our gente comes together—
our poetry, carnal."

First Floricanto was in '73,
November 13 and 14, just a year ago, at USC

That's where I met RaulrSalinas—the small r
is for Roy. Most of the time
he keeps this a secret.

He was just out of Leavenworth.
Red bandanna, Levi's *planchados,*
spit-shined *calcos,* and a black belt,
as thin as a toothpick.

Miguel Méndez and Tomás Rivera read
from their new *libros, Peregrinos de Aztlán*
and . . . *y no se lo tragó la tierra.*

They looked serious, even though
they still combed their *greña* like pachucos
especially Miguel,

wore formal
light-colored short sleeves too,
but I recognized the language, the tone,
what they were saying.

Teresa Palomo Acosta talked about
el Teatro de los Niños from Pasadena.
She was writing plays, poetry plays;
this hadn't been done before.

Veronica Cunningham was coming out
with her sexual politics, ahead of all of us.
She read

when all the yous
of my poetry
were really
she or her
and
i could never . . .

Veronica paused,

no
i would never
write them
because
of some fears
i never even wanted
to see.

Zeta Acosta,
the Brown Buffalo,

East Los, Raza Lawyer and
San Francisco nomad
(originally from the San Joaquín Valley)
stood up, asked the techs
to turn the theater lights off. Then
he read chapter 8 from his new
novel—
The Revolt of the Cockroach People.
About a Chicano,
named Robert Fernández,

"suicided"
by the L.A.P.D.,

a Chicano on a metal autopsy
table with nothing left, not even
face skin. Zeta lost the battle
with Noguchi, the coroner at the time
in Los Angeles—the body decomposed
case closed. Lack of evidence
on the Pacific edge of America.

That was the last time
I saw Zeta, his body blocked out
in black. Only voice, full of breath,
almost as if he was praying;
I noticed it when he read the last page
and asked Robert for forgiveness.

"Forgive me Robert,
for the sake of the living brown,"
Zeta said,
as if he was dying too.

Shortly after the festival
Zeta disappeared in Mexico;
off the coast of Michoacán, they say,
no one knows.

Austin was full of sky.
Instead of pyramids, there were clouds,
tints of green, sandstone, slate blue.

At U.T. Austin, we danced, I barely
knew the danzas, *la del Sol,* for example.
I forgot the names of the others. There
was one where we squat, keep the feet steady
then go into swift circles above the ground,
flesh spins, into lost centuries.

My legs whiter than *arroz con leche.*
Mario had the same problem.

If I could do it, he could do it.
If he did it, I did it.

Florencio didn't mind.
He liked the way we talked our Azteca history;
Indian books, Egyptian maps
salvaged from the San Diego Public Library
on "E" Street.

After the reading and performances
like the one Cecilio García-Camarillo
did using a tiny radio
and kung fu moves,
after Américo Paredes read on Sandino,
way after Reyes Cárdenas,
the only Chicano poet with *canas* at the time,
we ran into Tomás Atencio, a *cuentista*
from Peñasco, New Mexico.

Why don't you come up
to our pueblo and dance?
Seven thirty, in the town hall, he said.

Orale.

Two days later, we filled
the Mustang with more tuna
cracker tacos. The wind blew
our drums and luggage off the roof
on the way into Santa Fe.
Stuff was hanging off the side
for about twenty-five miles,
wind whipping the way forward.

Two hours late
but gente was still waiting, huddled
sombreros and long dresses.
So, Mario and me strapped on our *guitarras*
sang "El Picket Line"
and some songs we had written
together with Alurista.

Songs like "Vamos caminando
hacia la vida real," "Nubes de lucha,"
and "Altísimo corazón."

We were Okier than Hank Williams,
more organic than Maharishi Mahesh.

Florencio and the Aztec boys
were in the back of the wooden stage changing
their *ropa*. I could hear Piolín cuss,
said he couldn't fit
into his bikini pants
from all the *refín* in Austin. Refín
was the gift of the danzante, to celebrate
after small sacrifices, fasts, the giving
of oneself to the gods and goddesses
through one's body

made of roads,
clouds, rough sparrows—all in motion.

After the show, we ate
Sopaipillas, frijoles colorados con salsa
and *chicos con carne de res.*

We had never seen that kind of food.
Sopaipillas like erotic *quesadillas*
blown up and dipped in red
chile sauce from Chimayó. (If you box your
orejas right, they'll turn to sopaipillas.)

The *viejitas* from Chimayó
grow the *chiles colorados,* in front
of their painted adobe houses, they dry them;
nietos and *nietas* harvest them.

Chicos, baby corn kernels,
pearled yellow thorns that centuries ago turned
into sweet milk drops, translucent,
to cook in the frijoles
with fresh ground beef.

After this I wanted to stay in Peñasco.
But we kept on when Tomás said,

"You should look up Reggie Cantú, in Taos;
he's part of La Academia, you know.
He's up there with el Arnie Trujillo.
Están bien locos."

La Academia was like the Centro Cultural
in San Diego. A place in Peñasco
where the local artistas got their jales done,
in their own style, the *comunidad* walks in,
eats *cena* on the table, sings—
even el Loquito de Peñasco pushes his eyes up.

Tomás told us about el Reggie and el Arnold.
One was a poet and playwright, *el otro*
a photographer.

"Maybe they can get you some jales
in the schools while you're there,"
Tomás told us at the cena.

"Let's gotas," Conejo said.
"Let's gotas," I crooned.

Drive into Taos.
The first thing you notice
is that Taos is surrounded
by a ring of blue-colored mountains;
their journey ended there,

after one
long darkness when the universe became light.
Their bluish mist speaks of this.

They are sacred,
I remembered Tomás saying that.

That's where the Taos Indians
take the young boys so that they
can become men, with chants, admonishments,
the giving of pain inside the body,
their new eyes, sleepless moss at dawn.

They stay up there
fasting, praying,
finding their life.

We called Reggie from a gas stop
on a hill before we went into town.

The light was sharp on the stones.
Sagebrush, sky—

a lizard on a sparkling
dark rock, blowing in, blowing out.
We followed the trail for a while,
taking in the flavor of the red earth,
the invisible oil of the plants, we

looked down at Taos, open country,
Indian pueblos, reddish, brown, soft,
a favored cup of the wind gods.

Reggie, was a thin guy
with funny quickness
something like a Chicano Woody Allen,
a clean one. He took us to Anita Rodríguez's
cantón, a circular eight-room adobe house.

Anita was an *enjarradora,*
one who smoothes adobe clay on the inside,
follows its shape, into a hearth, a fireplace.

The inner sheath of her *casa*—a sand blanket
folded over the shape of the adobe
into a brownish bowl of sparkles,
the fire hole, where the fire shows itself
blue, red,
blue,

an earth-stone womb
made with her hands.

We stayed a few days,
ate good *tortillas de harina,* carried *leña,*
made fire in the morning,
fed *la estufa*—this house
kept us warm, outside the blue-powdered cape
was infinite snow.

We met Arnie, *el cuadrado*
with thick glasses.
He seemed to know the same stories
that Reggie knew,

about the pueblo *curandero,*
el viejito, Don Jaramillo, for example.

Reggie and Arnie made a few *visitas*
and got us invited to perform at Taos Junior High.

On the bleachers, the children
were clay brown, with clear eyes,
black torches of hair.

I had never seen Indios
and Chicanos at the same time,
sitting in the same row
looking like each other,
not even in the heights of Ramona.

This city of blue songs
taught me this was possible.

And their kindled voices: I could hear all their voices
with every step I took in the dance circle.

This was good. Something moved
inside me, a little above my stomach
pulling me forward, blowing sweetness
into my lungs, up to my forehead. The flavor
was in my mouth too.

The next day we danced at Taos Indian School,
then inside Taos Pueblo Church.

Wasn't sure about the church,
it was a sacred place for the Taos Pueblo people.

Who was I?
What was I?
What dance could I offer?
What was I carrying forward?
Did I have mysteries,
ancestors?

I had forgotten about shelter,
about seeking, all this, about
dreaming the way one asks questions,
to a sudden sparrow knocking.

Wasn't used to offering a dance
or even visiting.

Wasn't used to anything like this.
But I danced out of the lightness
that I carried inside.

Florencio said a few words to the elders,
very few, maybe he just smiled, gazed
into their eyes and they gazed back, bowed
their heads a little, in the dark, like birds.

Florencio walked in, barefoot
his headdress
and feathers, holding up the *incensario*
lit with sharp flecks of *copal.*

We followed the sweet smoke:
Piolín,
Lázaro,
Conejo,
Cerillo,
Mario, and Me.

We stepped through the blue roots,
the spirals of tree smoke copal
up to the Taos altar;

there was reddish corn,
star shapes in husk-leaf,
yellowish flesh, seeds in gourds, enameled
saucers, other figures, full of light,
didn't look directly at them,
I was dancing

a long way from home,
Austin in my blood, Peñasco
Velarde, Pojoaque, Española, the trails
that led me to this humble prayer house
my home was here, I could feel it

moving my legs, my belly tight
through the circle, we were

weaving our shoulders
through the wet darkness of the brown church
in step with the carved drum
inside greater circles,
blue mountains, blessing circles
above blue mountains.

Mariachi Drag Star

for the last zoot-suiters
of the world

Air guitar on Lincoln Blvd.
Call me Freddy this time. Freddy B. Good in mariachi drag.

Got my father's grape-picking knife, the one with a hooked blade dangling from my
sequined belt made in Jalisco, a wavy turf that takes you into the sky and drops you
on a flatbed mango truck. Hauling fast. You have to see my boots. Like the ones my
uncle Beto sent me when I was five years old living on the outskirts of Escondido.
See me bomb the anthills in my chopper—a can of kerosene in one hand, a match
in the other, my left one. There I am chewing grapefruit, sitting on a wooden bench,
the meat is diced and spiced with sugar and cinnamon. My feet stick out. The little
spiral arabesque designs by the ankles can barely be seen. And my pants—this is
what counts and makes me loose: velveteen black canvas drapes, used for Elvis
Presley or John F. Kennedy posters and sold a few blocks down, at La Fulton mall.
And my shirt. It hasn't changed. Have a "Boycott Coors" and a "Boycott Grapes" and
"U.S. out of El Salvador" and "Apartheid" buttons running down the sides of my
embroidered sleeves. The hat really is the best item. Size of a New York pizza, with
a gourd for the head. Bought the gourd on Olvera Street where the artists hang out
and go to blues shows at night. That's all they have here is blues shows. My face is
rusty. This is the way I look when I swagger down the avenues. Say things like fuck

a duck *cabrón,* I am a Capricorn. Sometimes they rhyme like that. Malls are my hangouts. Cross-legged on the linoleum in Radio Shack to tease the store manager. Where are your radios? Or slide by the Mitsubishi dealer and push the color intensity to black on the 40-inch demonstration model. I am deep inside now. Standing next to the *licuados*—Indian energy drinks made out of local weeds. *Chilacayote* and *flor de calabaza.* Flor de calabaza is good for hangover quesadillas and chilacayote is a cure-all especially if you happen to get poison ivy *pito* or as they say in English, poison ivy dick. This is what beaner men get when they mess with their genitals while hiking around Topanga Canyon in cutoff Friscos. Chicano men always dress the same whether they are at the beach or in the mountains: cutoff black Friscos with ragged Fruit of the Loom T-shirts. It has nothing to do with class or gender. The women are more creative.

Believe me, I know about poison ivy. When I was a kid, I got a bad case of *chile huero* pito. This time it was the yellow wax pepper that did me in. What a mess. My mom had to yank me out of the trailer and haul me over to a *tina,* an extra-large tin bucket in the middle of the dirt yard next to the killing post used for wild turkey on special Saturdays. My father, Emilio, did that stuff.

Now I am next to a fashionable men's store, a European joint that sells French tweeds with orchid ties. Six hundred to fifteen hundred dollars. These are starting prices.

I spin to a foreign tune; Trini López sings Farsi in my head. Milling my arms round and round doing a disjointed hula, skating up the granite and onyx open-air restaurant floors. There is a man whispering to an oval-faced Mexican Penelope. His reddish face looks up and down at her from his tiny seat. Two white dudes shuffle into the sports shop where two black vatos are holding up a Bull's jacket. Moving fast.

My leathery heart burns up its last jelly drop. I sing—picking grapes the way my father did. Pull up my Roman-nosed knife. Same shape as my nose. Passolini strolling to the Caracalla baths in Rome. Waltzing through the mud, holding a little boy's hand while he pulls a Ducati bike with the other. The mother in a greenish tunic looks on at me in the rain. Her hands go up and rest at the hips. I pull the bike faster than the other kid next to me. He is wearing the same outfit. Where did he get it? Maybe it's my lost brother. The one whose hands they would tie to the pews at St. Ann's. The brother I thought I always had. The one that likes kosher pickles and peanut butter burritos. And who's that below him? She is rolling on the ground. She is uncontrollable, bursting with tears of laughter or is it sweat? No, she's laughing. I don't know her. I don't want to look at her. Whose sister would wear headphones in this heat? You can hear Wilson Pickett's jagged falsetto belting out of her ears. To my left, a Filipino man is hoeing. Fast. Red cap and striped canvas gloves. He is anxious. Looks like my father. I recognize the nerves.

Bobbing and weaving. Skating. Burning ants.

Luring the juice out from the bulbous violet fruit. My spurs are somewhere, tumbling below the skylights.

My spurs emit little swishing sounds so I won't lose my step. I am falling. This is downtown Venice. I 've been here for ages, it seems. Next to La Cabaña Café, the place I have bumped into. I am in there, drinking coffee and eating a caraway cheese sandwich with bologna from Chicago. My cigarette burns and spits a spark. Sister Leila comes out of the back in her woolly brown skirt. She reminds me it is time to go to work at Ellison Tire. Look out the window—there is a guy spilling his snow cone trying to figure where he's headed. His legs shoot out from under him into the glassy street. His face wiggles too, like Fred Flintstone, like the rest of us. Picks at a tiny address book in his shirt pocket, the one thing his mother left him wrapped in a rum-colored scarf before she died. Now, he rubs his finger on it, reads it like a novel.

NIGHT
TRAIN
TO
TUXTLA

Zeta

late 1989

Zeta Mendoza is dead. I left him doubled up in a small cornfield in Panama, somewhere near the Costa Rican border. That's all there is to say about it. No one knows this except me.

Larkin Street San Francisco drink joint.

This is where it's at for the moment. Light up a cigarette, buddy, gaze at the descent of the matchstick as it twists toward the floor. Look up at the bartender and then look away; remember the city back in the fifties, the way Zeta did.

Boy, he used to say—

you couldn't sport a finer gabardine jacket with Daisy Robles going up to the Orpheum on Easter Sunday or the Black Hawk—listen to Cal Tjader on vibes and Desmond on sax. You see, everything was in the shape of a fancy sparkle; even the question mark by her telephone number in my pocket calendar or the last note scribbled on a table napkin. It was all personality, black coffee and music.

Black Hawk, I whisper—

and feverishly drink down the tiny glass of bitter syrup in my hand. I look around. Greasy smiles.

Electric peanuts in the sky—I laugh to myself.

Zeta used to say that about the lights above the Bay Bridge. Kill time. Say anything that comes to your mind, just make sure you forget Zeta's twisted body. In San Francisco, you'll forget.

Just gotten off the Golden Gate bus half a block away. I was wired.

December afternoon outside, wind cooling. Another drink at Tony's tavern on the corner of Larkin and Geary. Outside: downtown archways, stone alleys—a kid with french fries and sauce leaking through the bag jumps at the curb.

The mirror behind the bartender betrays me. I stroke my right ear; I feel awkward. I was never this thin, so bluish—maybe too much left back there in the crazy tropics. Take a bus to the beach just like when you were a downtown boy. Yeah.

As the bus left Market Street, looking at the kid wind up a staircase to his apartment, I think of my mother still in her tiny room without an escape ladder on Mission Street. The extra-large jar of Jergen's night cream on her wicker basket altar. Saints she prays to, offerings she makes.

Muni pier looms ahead. Walk up the concrete coil where Chinese women huddle by the cold benches rigging up crab net. Hook an eel with the pole.

▪ ▪ ▪

"Look, López, there's a lot going on. The military are swarming all over the place. This government is out to get Noriega one way or another, he knows too much, you know—all the fucking hanky-panky these white ambassadors have been pulling for years in Central America. Buying women. Hauling coke. Arms and champagne. I was at the college meeting the other day and some of the people that got smuggled in last week across the border said everything is hot out there. You know what I mean, man.

"I am fucking tired of just looking at people getting screwed one way or another. Can't sleep, can't paint. Can't even screw right. Gotta go out there, check it out; I don't know, you want to come?" He was serious.

"You're crazy, Zeta, in Central America if you are Indian looking, young, and carrying a book, you're dead meat! I can't even speak Spanish right, shit." He came back at me, "What's the problem, bro?"

I smiled a wilted smile. Then his face darkened, his jaw seemed to shift, widen.

"López, we gotta go. The scene here stinks. Everyone is out for your jugular. The murals I painted back in '79 are washed out. Nobody seriously reads anything—even if the paper is on fire, they'll just lay it down and walk away to their stucco houses. What am I supposed to do now—apply for a candy-assed grant to paint an alley like the rest of the so-called artists around here? My tag is up in every alley all the way to Oakland. Nobody's crossed it out. You know why? You wanna know? Because they ain't got no guts and no souls, man! This city is dead. The people are dead and everything they are doing right now this very minute is dead. Got it?"

"Yeah," I half-mumble. I look out to the Transcontinental Tower jutting from the heart of Chinatown into the weak sky. On the shore, a few hunched lovers examine the sand for the first time, picking up shiny stones that will fade as soon as they dry. Yeah, right.

■ ■ ■

Daisy—yes, Zeta wanted her; she was good to him and now she was gone. He liked to make up pictures of both of them, draw them for me in his beat-up sketch pad on the way south through Tegucigalpa, Honduras: Think of a romantic movie in the fifties, rum-colored bandannas and jukeboxes.

In the middle of Dolores Park, I was the guy with baggy corduroys doing a tango. Me and Daisy and her Portuguese accent. She was the only real dancer at one hundred twenty-two degrees west longitude, baby.

Daisy was out of the picture now. The art scene in San Francisco was a billboard inferno. Everything from Haight Ashbury to Daly City had been whitewashed and glossed with glitter and New Age Asians and Hispanics running for office. Zeta used to say a crazy demolition team had come in overnight and left us with six-story parking lots, bad cars, the elegant bold type of murder in the daily newspapers, frenzy pills, cut-out military episodes from Nam pasted over with apologia and mirror bank buildings.

One night, after his last art opening at the Galería de la Raza on Bryant Street, Zeta came up to me—a drink in his hand: "López, all we have is a little kit—a few things like soap and toothpaste, a pair of odd-matched socks; well-packed bundles under our shirts, pearlike shapes of rage, desire and lonesome dreams."

A little kit—I wasn't good with words like Zeta.

I can still hear Zeta. I can't get over it:

"Remember my mom? Yeah, you remember," he said. "Remember how she used to cook us *caldo de res* after a whole weekend of us carousing, reading poems, getting drunk, and thinking we were being political. Come on, how she looked at us— as if we were young and strong, full of fresh smells, smiles, and medals; ready to walk all the way downtown for a riot with the cops at the snap of a finger, a phone call, anything. That look she gave us, man. We were losing something. We were the old lost ones, weren't we?"

∎　∎　∎

I decided to leave for Central America with Zeta. Sure did. I was better off in Panama, maybe. I always ended up doing whatever Zeta got into, anyway. At city college, he used to hang around the teachers after class talking about astrology, Sartre, and French films. French films? Never even had French bread. So, I went along. Never said a thing. Nothing. Just kinda smiled. One time even gave everyone a penny. Didn't know what to do or say. Just gave them a penny. Then, at school: *Thus Spake Zarathustra* on my desk in chemistry lab. My mom was scared, she thought I was getting into devil stuff. It all worked itself out, somehow. Follow Zeta, it's OK, it told me, this thin stuff here inside my gut. Zeta is right, it said.

"I'll tell you about the *marine thing* later, man." Zeta was throwing his arms up, pulling at his goatee, swiveling his shoulders, loose, striding, as we stepped out of the wrinkled wagon-bus we had boarded in the open-air depot back in Guatemala City. Later: "They say Edgar hasn't been seen in weeks." Zeta looked concerned as he hung up the phone outside the main plaza in Tegucigalpa. Edgar was a guy on the inside of things—an accountant by day, a sentry for the Left by night.

The white colonial towers bounced light through the trees. I was spinning. Heat thickened the fragrance of the budding flowers. In the plaza, a half-naked boy tumbled over a towel sprinkled with glass slivers. Another blew out fire from his mouth, eyeing the *turistas* rushing by looking for hotels, cigarettes, taxis.

By nightfall, we had ended up in Panama City, stopped at a cafe. Zeta mumbled something about trekking twenty-five kilometers further south. We rested and smoked. Then he made a call and got directions to Edgar's place in the hills. Edgar would fill us in—we were close, he said.

In the morning we found Edgar barely alive in a small village.

∎　∎　∎

I thought about all this on the pier.

∎　∎　∎

Crawling through the smoking corn slush, pushing my boots down on the blackened sod, then Zeta found Edgar ahead of me. Bullets burned in his right thigh. A gaping hole by his shoulders. Edgar was dreamy and spurted words as best as he could, pointing ahead to a river. The villagers had fled to the border river, he said.

Old farmers, women, and children shot down by American soldiers—Edgar kept on repeating this and pointed again; there had been helicopters. Zeta went further. He disappeared and then came up holding the hand of another body along the field.

It was raining—hard rain smashing the wide, red-flared plant leaves along the small roads. I could hear the mad ticking all around and inside of me. The sky lowered and then unraveled its dark knots that had been tightening since dusk and then, thunder. All the tiny things in the earth below were loosening with a music of their own—little bones in water letting go of their cargo. Suddenly, all around us, the cornfields whitened in a sharp, strange light, a pure light. Zeta! His arms came up, caught in a storm of flickering sheaths, little blazing shards, his face slowly going to the side and the torso—stretching, curling at the edges, the thousand brilliant translucent shells falling to his feet—in a millisecond, not far from me; I lost Zeta to this light. I ran to Edgar and told him I would come back with help.

I I I

I can still hear the lightning.

I 've been pacing every walkway in San Francisco for the last two weeks thinking about this. Been drinking too much Yukon Jack syrup. Yesterday, it took me two hours to get out of the house—lost the keys in my sweatshirt, left the door open, got back and thought my cassette player had been stolen. Then, remembered I had pawned it for more fast food, cigarettes, and sweet drinks.

Standing.

Thinking in the middle of the street. Shotwell Avenue. Zeta's last mural. I look to the Southern sky and try to make the connection between Zeta's crazy acrylics—the swirling elongations of arms, robes, the fleshy ochre whiteness, even the piety of the hands as they reach up toward something dark and unknown—and my last image of him.

There was nothing that could be done in Panama.

I I I

I wandered back—caught buses. Bummed money from old pals in Mexico City. Made it to Mexicali to pick up the Chevy we had parked before catching a train. It was slouched over a ravine by the train station. The seats were littered with orange sandwich papers, diapers, and soiled pillows. I dumped the papers and diapers and a knot of newspapers that was stuffed into the door to keep out the cold air. Filled up one of the tires with air and made it to Escondido, California. Bummed more gas money and a dinner from Gabby Vásquez, a good buddy of mine who is the only decent person I know that is happily married—three kids and a wife named Rosemary. In his house there was a filmy kind of stream making everything moist: the wood grain on the door, the television's blackish rubbery plastic molding. Even Rosemary. Her lips porous, the hair on her arms longer, lighter. Having another baby, going to name him Toño, she said. Gabby gets up early. Pulls out his jump rope with a black ball at the end of each cord. Five hundred, he says. Five hundred. I open my hands to my side, tighten my fingers two or three times, then close them into a fist and leave for San Francisco in one straight drive, loop into downtown where the green and silver windows block out everything the sun gives except the abstract noise shooting up from the asphalt. I park the Chevy on Polk, walk away still seeing patches of the cornfield in front of me—uprooted in yellowish brown heaps and the waxy faces and shoulders falling out of the bloody slush. And the brilliant lights crashing on Zeta.

My mother once told me about what happened before we moved to San Francisco. I was a child and my father, Emilio, was working the tractor as a farmhand out on the edge of town bordering Arizona. The immigration patrol had snared three Mexicans without papers. They were taunting them and from a large reserve can poured gasoline on one of the men. My father never told anyone else about it. The immigration officers would blame him, he said. He would rub his face hard when he said this, then turn away.

It was getting late. The streets were hurting me—pacing in squares and zigzags, leaning on little restaurant walls I had never visited. My face against the windows. See the thick coats hunched over a bowl of soup, the nervous hands flipping the basket for more French bread. A waitress chewing gum grimaces at a wino who steps in and shoves a menu into him like a knife. Couples with their tiny pink pastry boxes in a bag hang their coats and wait for a glass of water to wash things away. My stomach churns, I tap my cigarette pack against the fleshy part of my palm and light one, slowly eyeing the furniture specials on the street.

The furniture stores still put up the same old Christmas sale signs, I chuckle sourly.

I thought of Zeta and Edgar. There was nothing I could do about Edgar. I told the villagers to go for him. What more could I do?

Central America was always hot. We said it—over a wine cooler or at a poetry reading in the Mission District. None of us would even dare leave San Francisco. And any fire-play out there gave us more reason to stay put.

I couldn't get back into the city—no matter how much I tried to dig into the concrete. Just couldn't get back.

Days are at a standstill. Papers say Noriega lives in the Vatican embassy now—listens to heavy metal blasting from the marine's speakers. He doesn't want to show his face.

∎ ∎ ∎

The old deli had a dim light on. It was a greenish two-story Victorian that stood on the corner facing a Bekins storage facility—maybe the last Bekins building in the Mission District; U-Haul was taking over. Further up, a closed beer brewery was being torn down. People said the city was going to build a school there later in the year. The rest of the block was boarded up except for a few smaller houses scattered here and there. It was very late now. What could I say to Zeta's mom?

I pushed the little button again and again.

"It's me, Señora Mendoza."

I heard a young man's voice with a funny accent. I tried to think where to start. "Victor?" I said hoping it was Zeta's brother as the door opened.

I wanted to say more but, I couldn't. Vic said nothing, as he limped ahead passing the black deli refrigerators towards the back room. I could see the *coquitos* on display by the juices—we used to wrap them in cellophane on weekends so Zeta's dad could sell them to the Mexican candy stores in the District. I smelled candles, medicine, and the coconut oil in the candy. The smell of burnt corn stumps came up. My stomach loosened. "Vic?" I peeped again.

"Victor?" I was louder this time. Nothing came back.

I only had seen him a few times, at dinner or going out with his friends. Now, he wasn't very big; he was frail, the box of his shoulders tight, tiny. Angular face, unshaven; a religious air. Before I could ask him anything, he opened the door to an amber-lit room and just said, "He's waiting for you."

Another silence.

Nothing came back from me this time. I was stopped by the odd breathing coming from the man sitting on a makeshift bed in front of me. "He's been waiting for you."

I turned to an old woman at the end of the bed. She moved her lips without looking at me.

Zeta's dead. I left him in Panama. A mortar shell burned him alive. I saw it. All this balled up in my throat and left me speechless. I couldn't say this now. There was nothing I could say. Who was this man? Zeta's mother knelt at the foot of the crooked mattress. I turned to Vic standing by the door. But he motioned with his thin hand, shooing me back.

Zeta's breath was swimming through his lungs. Remember? I thought to myself: the gnarled forehead, things fluttering across his face. "Come on, Zeta," I said. Blinking fast, his eyes watered, glaring at mine. His mouth opened and closed trying to make something inside speak. But he couldn't make it work. The tongue moved and pushed. All I could see were the damn blisters at the back, by the tonsils. And he closed his eyes, dropped his head.

"What happened?" The strange man spoke with an odd childlike swing to his voice.

"Yes?" I said, awkwardly. He glared. Zeta's mom nodded and stood up propping one hand on the bedside and walked over to the dresser and handed me a letter.

I was sweating. Raised a hand and brushed my hair with my fingers. All this had already done something to alter her quiet poise. The envelope did more. She stood far away and pointed the letter at me. I moved up to her, took the note and heard myself saying: "Gracias, Señora Mendoza." A muffled fear trembled in the corners of her eyes. She was turning her eyes toward the suited man, then little Vic. Then at me. I stood there looking at her, there in the dark box, burning with an old bulb on the high ceiling. I started to open the envelope.

"Not now, López." I turned to the man. He was sullen. Serious.

"What do you mean, *not now?*"

"Not now, I said."

"Is this about Zeta?" I stammered. "I need to know what's in this letter."

"You never made it to Panama, OK?"

He brushed the stubble on his chin. I wanted to put it in my shirt pocket, but nothing moved.

"You went on a vacation, maybe Acapulco; an old buddy looked you up, maybe."

"What?"

"You saw nothing, punk." He says and he jumps up to me.

"*You saw nothing, OK?* Or maybe you were running cocaine for the military back there? Maybe you've been doing this for two years now. You and Mr. Zeta. What else could two college dropouts do to keep up with things in the city? And maybe you sold some to your artist friends, you know the ones that wear all those 'Apartheid' and 'U.S.A. out of El Salvador' buttons? I got it all here in my notes." He laughs, walking around the bed.

"And then you know what?" Pokes me. "Why don't you ask Mrs. Mendoza and Vicky boy? They're smart."

He reaches inside his his coat behind his worn leather belt and pulls out a snub-nosed gun. Waving it in a short, nervous circle, planting it on my right temple.

"Let us say it was going pretty good for a while. You started making fine drug money, eating fine—better than hanging around Berkeley selling rings with the rest of the weirdos. Then you know what?"

He was getting louder. "Your buddy Zeta got an idea: more stuff. Right? But, he didn't have the connections. So you guys went south." He was breathing hard. "You saw nothing, López." He stalled, backed off, stopped: He was sorting things out, shuffling his story into my story—how I smuggled stuff back to the streets and how he could prove it in one easy sweep, how I had seen the American military kill one of our own, and how he would pin me so I would stay quiet—he glanced at Zeta's mom, then at me. He brought up the gun again and pointed me towards the little door.

He was pushing me out of the room with the gun at my back. I wanted to turn around and grab at something. Zeta's mom was stiffening, opening her mouth try-ing to push something out, wheezing, pulling up the bones in her shoulders. She ran up to the headboards and dropped next to the bed.

"Come on, get out, I don't need you." He closed the back door with his free hand. Then he picked up a sandwich by the refrigerator door and took a sumptuous bite. "You say something and I'll get her too, Señor López." A hot bitter liquid came up my throat.

I wanted to turn back to the cornfields, run back through the wetness. The *mass graves*—up there by the cornfields—the American military had them dug in al-ready, just waiting for the air attack on Panama City. A set up. I was frozen.

He pushed me by the head out the front door onto the street. Something came over me. I jammed my arm through the closing edge of the door lock, grabbed it, and pressed back. I was backing him up now.

"Come on, mister, shoot my brains out." I was talking fast.

"Get the hell outta here, López."

"And then what you gonna do, shoot the candies?"

"Shut up!" He was moving further back. A bit more every time.

"*You* didn't see nothing." I pushed him.

Zeta's mom was moaning in the closed room. "Blow me away, buddy." My voice was coming from deep down. "You want to know what that letter says?" He barked, shielding the door to the little room. "Go ahead, let's see it, pull it out—let's hear about your *vacation*." He waved his little gun again.

I held up a picture: a couple of guys with a woman in fancy clothes, snorting powder on the table—drinks, aperitifs, musicians in blue-vested suits. "Who's going to believe this crap—this guy don't even look like me. Zeta had straight hair." I wanted to tear the photos, shred them, and fling the pieces at him. Didn't say a word, just stood there, dropped the glossies on the floor. Squinting and wiping the side of my face, turned around and didn't look back. Walked out. "You saw nothing," he whispered. "Don't come back, López, I swear . . ." he went on as I shut the front door. It was around four in the morning. The steel street signs above me.

∎   ∎   ∎

Moving off down the curb, Zeta talks into my ear—how one day he couldn't sell his uncle's landscape paintings at the market. No one was buying them anymore. Right? All of a sudden nobody wanted bulls and gallant, lean young kids in shimmering bronze suits on their walls. Now, it was all about abstract portraits. Squares. Upside-down eyes.

Night Train to Tuxtla

The heavens above me
black clouds blending with the white ones.
Margarita Luna Robles

Downslope, sleek concrete.

Blurred gate at La Central in D.F. This is where you bring your bags and cardboard,
leave behind a sack of viscera. It's not going to help you cross over. La Central:
the wooden hub of brown exiles dressed in rubber; bound south. Some prefer the
East. Prefer the South where you can breathe in broken pieces of sweat music. Billie
Holliday and her velveteen dress waves from above, frocked in a Virgen de Guada-
lupe shawl. Stars, marimbas, sex, and moon shafts. She drops it on the man ahead
of me, the guy with a herringbone comb in his hip pocket, the guy, with a news-
paper jammed in his short sport coat, flying. We are all running. No one looks up
toward Billie nude and coming softly with her arms open and her mouth singing
her last song. We think it's behind the windows. The ruffled heat under our collars,
inside the T-shirt. An old woman in a jersey print leaps through an aisle and grabs
a seat. Three students roll into each other and press through the angled doors drop-
ping books and a canteen full of vodka and grape soda. Before I get there, the train
fills. Jump in, a tiny woman screams, and I crash on the crooked floor with the rest
of the band. The night explodes and the wheels churn in the rain. The old woman
has curled a giant ball out of rags and presses it into her stomach, bows her head.
The man next to me with his back facing me says his name is Macedonio. He corrects

me and says its Colonel Macedonio. Worked the sugar mills in Veracruz for twenty years, got cancer in the liver. Just back from *la clínica* in D.F., he says. We exchange a few sighs and elbow each other for air. The storm presses against the glass. The black veins squirm and the moist steel and plastic leather rock us to sleep. My wife, says another. She left. Didn't want to make love one afternoon; she called me a thief, rented an old Cadillac and took off for Morelia. The next day a white kitten in the yard knocked down a slab of plywood and smashed its own head, it wanted to live, for a while. Macedonio laughs. He's got his money wound in his socks. Glass socks he mumbles, bought them at the San Antonio bazaar. A man with a little green suitcase pulled them out, twisted them and lit one up with a match. Then, he stabbed it with a stiletto. Glass, he said. When will we get to Tuxtla? One of the students dressed in Adidas jogging pants says the best shopping malls are in Tuxtla—Gala, Gala, she whispers the name of the place to her girlfriend. We are headed downward. Going into a deeper spin. A darker sleeve of the ocean where the steel wheels turn into sea anemones and the conductor speaks a dolphin language. We are all floating in the mid-levels of the waters, holding each other hand in hand, except my hands can't feel the fingers. Something fluttering and porous is at the end of my right foot. Fall in, into a skull-shaped pit at the bottom. There is a bottom now. A crescent of starfish at the edges play with a bulbous growth. Can barely see. They are building a new hotel in Tuxtla too. Fiesta Americana, the girlfriend whispers back. After you leave the station you can feel it as you come into town. On the hill. And the Indian soldiers stand with their automatics. Upright, chromed. At the entrance to every boutique.

Tatarema

The bones curve out from the shoulders
into the earthwalls, passages, fifty thousand workers,
sugary discs carried on the back, absent among the shrouds,
only stones, stones upon skull with a thin sheath,

a black hive, Sierra Pelada
gold mines, unforgivable skin, Brazilian,
and there are mouths again, up

through the sod, the broad-hipped caves in the hill, a factory,
a vein-digging chasm, hospitals with old women in torn muslin,
the kind you see in dreams, scorched, greenish, shredded,
this shawl—

in Sertão de Bahia, the 24-year-old bride scratches the back
of a rock, sits in a '61 Rambler station wagon slammed by a truck, engine on,
overlooking the vanishing road, overlooking the sand, chalk dust

on her cheekbone, she wears
a white carnation and the ribbon unwinds on her knees,
ship-breakers,

coal-burning roofers, I am calling you, with your transport—
the heavy steel gash from Bangladesh, remember Bangladesh,

back in '71 someone cried for you,
hailed you and sang to you, I call again, naked without a hat,
if you wander

without a leg long enough, someone will find you and meet you
at the *milpa* with a Holy Crane-shaped cloud above you, the left hand up
as if holding a witch's white veil,

uncovering the dead of the church, disinheritance—to say it for once,
even if in this text, even if your eyes are hard, eating cold,

from the dented steel bowl, with a shadowy spoon,
with your hands at the waist at the end of the sugarcane day
cutting the rust from your night face,

come with a beard, with a shirt rolled and a fist wrapped,
and a stream of banana leaf and the feet with a barbed pick in the earth,
I am not describing the subject,

this is not the subject, dear reader, the ceramic baby in shards,
not skin anymore, kneeling again, again, yes—kneeling
at the handmade canal,

bricks without milk and the woman's bosom
wrapped in a hotel blanket left long ago,

a Bush maid under contract again, with the belly
streaming, coal soot and penniless, the hearth beaten down to the tin,
it is not unusual,

it is not unusual to write this,
remember that if you wish,

there is a wicker basket with a stone balanced on the head, a cotton plant
splayed against the air—history, someone says, this is how you learn to walk,
there is a canvas waiting for you, yes, for you,

the dunes, the white shroud I spoke of,
an olive cut open inside the eye and the hand waving
good-bye, tied to a wire,

a medical chart for tuberculosis—refugee, you,
say it—refugee in a camp against the tree full of triumph over you,
the cactus with loud courage over you too, claws and shadows
again (so many shadows), two men praying—in their seventies,

wearing white again, also a soiled gurney floats
against the side wall of the village, woven by hand, perhaps
the children passing time, thinking of the sea—

one body at a time, here is the triumph you were asking for,
a gunny sack, knotted, muslin again, this spotted film the body wears
when it is flayed, there's a junkyard lacking wood, a steering wheel
shoots up from the heap, a mother wants it for her child,

maybe it will roll to heaven, maybe it will turn to music,
then flies, a loaf of bread and then, a city—for once,

a shaft inside the bluish rock, jutting its face into a fender, halfway,
tombstones made of coral and a boy thinking like this,

like this, yes—in a room, alone, thatched
roof again, crosshatched by the Sun Gods it is said, tied up to the ankle,
the boy's own camouflage from himself—leprosy, he wanders too
in this half-light, inside the closets,

the child half into the woman,
her legs stretched out against the Coptic floor,
an Ethiopian dispensary, yes, in a different shape from ours,
another shroud,

a warehouse of shrouds this time, empty, bitten sand, coffee cans,
tents, ten thousand pushing against the Korean mountain, big-bodied
women and men, oblong, they hear about food,

so they march, with a cane shoot and a folded rubber sack,
folded at the knuckles, shaving the skin—for a moment, the children pose
for a burial ceremony, the wheeze of the elders rises,

one shows her buck teeth, hiding behind a jagged slate
Sertão de Paraiba and crisscross the forehead, with the eyes
up in half-moon,

lost, holy Tarahumaras, speaking a word or two, famished, coppery
by the twig house, a child, again,

with candy-colored yarns in her hair, another marriage—think of this,
another marriage in the yards,

the man with a labyrinth tie and a game on the inside floor,
a bone game for the Great Wars—Tatarema—about to come,

what will protect you?
Open your arms

as if diving into leaves, the grave, the parted rag door in your house,
and the Holy Spirit on the last days of the year, dovelike, crosslike

with a jawbone and a healing stick above the lattice,
there is a bus stop too, in Huautla de Jiménez,

two withered dogs lying on a flour sack, empty, slates again, a candle,
a vase with an explosion of black and the caress of a child, a boy this time
on the way to a carnival,

there is a delivery to the village, a visit to the blind aunt,
a reddish patch that must be healed, a blanket of tiny rocks
and a violin, thick necked, festive,

an open gate of wooden trunks caught upside down,
emptying a few dance skirts, a military cap, in the back yards,

two boys and a girl with a palm leaf on her head,
ready for burial—looking steadily

now, yes—only now
there is time for that,

the cactus winds up its hair, glistens for a second
inside the spine, the oxen taste the plow and the mineral mountain
slips back into the wound,

the pewter mine in Oruro, Bolivia, the men unshaven
with their hands hidden from each other, three women dancing,
a tuba with a gaping lung, blue and black, a red screen,

a vapor, again, curling, and a clarinet on the table,
it is so still, so cold, this table where the mason and the wind carve a rose,
then, the glance of the dead goat, the flowers, tiny
oval tortillas and the chicken, headless over a colored pastel plate—

the eyelids, stretched, again, almost oiled,
clouds with their mother faces turned toward us, the mother

infested with crazy, moving lines above the brow and her melting eyes,
holding, reaching, mantislike, she wears a hat too,

a boiling tin pot held up by a weight scale for oranges, pushing
through the God sounds,

fifty thousand Indians, you could call them all
and they would turn to you and they would point with clay stub arms,
a dingy shoe, leaning against a single plank, almost a cross, a hull
for a boat used for welding,

according to a plan, determined, overdetermined
by the engineers, wait, don't let that word—engineers—guide you here,
it is meaningless, better say electrical cables, a furnace,

always a furnace in a brown room with goggles or with a dog
abandoning the village, the highest regions across the horizon, uncertain,
graceful, cameralike.

One Is for Maáx, One Is for Jabalí

for the people of Najá village,
Lacandón Rain Forest, Chiapas, México

This unknown fountain. Fifteen Mayas
from Lacanjá. Two from the village of Najá.

The wind on black print tunics. Designs
from the new mestizo factory.

They sit here,
by my knees, in wetness.

A last pin still turns the threads and speaks
for the useful water inside my broken cup.

One of them carries a chrome radio, clings
to the numbers: 5, 6, 7, 8, 9, 9, he leans, he sings

Pixán
Pixán

for tomato
for heart.

An ambush gives them away. I can't tell
if it was yesterday or centuries ago—
blood liquor,

Protestant oils, cheap perfume on the red beans
of the night necklace.

They keep to themselves when they carry this.
They touch a dying bird and speak of the color green.

My blood is this color,
with a full jaw, they say.

I can resist them. I run back to my
anguish and repel the heat, the cotton beak of the sky
comes to face me and I deny it.

The Lacandón Maya boys swing their legs
to one side, to the side of vastness and genocide.

No banquets
on their swollen glands,

the voluptuous mouth of Chan K'in José
as he stands near the la Ruta Maya, new road
to the Pemex oil plant, a few miles northwest

up the hill
where the lorry drops Tzeltal Indians.

In their rose skins, with machetes
they dig for the last *caoba* seed, they pull cans and glass.
By the ledge, underneath *la tiendita*

young Nuk sells bloated whips of sugar
and aspirin. She dissolves behind a ragged curtain.
Chan K'in José, in the back, chips and smoothes
a stone point.

He feels the swiftness of the flecked edge;
because the sky brings me secrets
from the trees, he says.

And everyone listens
with love and fullness, a scar on blue ground.

At midnight, with straight bamboo,
one meter. Wound with smoke wax string,
the arrows are ready.

One is for Maáx, for Howler Monkey.
One is for Jabalí, for deceiving boar.

They will come alone
to your walkway, near the parched stones of Palenque,
waveless, half of the world in light.

Memoria(s) from an Exile's Notebook of the Future

Crucé la frontera cargada de dignidad.
                                    Rigoberta Menchú

It took me long to walk
to this slate, a desert star,
pinned on my forehead, here,
in this brilliant stone rail,
carrying what was given
in sand and pouches
with all my familiars, in rough
kinship, occupied
without a returning spring,
through the sandal bones,

in puzzles, the quake-lined crops,
the picker songs, the passport designed on the neck,
the citizen language,
I speak of Genesis

between my mother and me, between my father
and me,
tear gas gauze, supplications
and her tiny ancient voices

and his long biblical compassions, factories
of dislodged pigments, blue muslin settlements,
a Moroccan tarp
through the short sickle years, the portioned
tomato days, the sliced sugar-cans
in the yard, left
with the imprint of six interrogators,
the doomed pellets

in the hourglass, working the wicked man's yard,
scrubbing and praying
in bone through the village bowl,
all night singing Yemeni songs falling astute
inside the floor, with the knees mapped,

my mother in
her apron condemned, my father
in his long coat of dust,
in his Turkish *baglame* shuffle, a sigh without
the tragedy of passage, this honorable wicker hat,
this merciful Jerusalem open hand, this dead

contract on the shoulders to the skull fields,
to the circular concrete, three columns of army jeeps,
the acrid sweetness at the center,
a mother hand waving,

a slanted apartment, number nine, number four,
number 14,
number this, number again, with salt, with blood
in tins with lost brine, from the last to the first pay stub,
counterclockwise

with the hands in, occupied,
with the house up in shock,

a bread roll behind the back, through the crazy sod,
in the tyrannical bar, a child with a meager landscape,
in the match basement
with all my wonderings, in patches,

red, green, and black, without the cloud colors,
without the vowel for an *A*,

for an *E*,
for *E*,
for *U*,
for *O*,
oval for oval sky,

to hang against the petty bureaucrats,
a poor-girl oasis, reflected

at night, to hold in the proud cell, in the eye,
in the ragged arm, her riddled back upright,
his squatted back
upright, your father through the tawdry rope,
through the gnarled vine, the hook knife,
the piece of rain pasted,
a raisin held in the fist, a razor bread, listen,

if you get out

as a night stranger, if you get out face first
there will be air and tobacco, then sing of Istanbul
and Old Jaffa, sweat on the skin,

air, reddish seeds and a ghost full of kinship,
a potter's wheel and a mason's table,
a few friends,
all in a concrete circle, broken or healed, a wound
from the tin boot and a chin strap reflected,
the stub writing,

the short ceiling, the cabbage soup,
a crash of blue maize
in the skillet, in the icebox bundle, my shadow,
my indigo wire,
full of sayings, thirteen days of crucifixions,
in a child's mad combat, the village heart

in the cloth, wrapped, something
about you, something about us, about
this sediment heat, terrible
in its long scarf, in its counterclockwise sheets,
a sky flame and an ash trumpet, caught
on the street sign,

an isolated unit, one last smoke,
tear gas in the coffee cans,
the eyes full of love and a newspaper stabbed
in the mouth, a knife in the shape of a tunnel,
where there is a bag of acorns for the road
ahead, black tea,

I am walking, like this,
in an oval, broken,

cloud healed, in the match gallery,
the canvas is nailed
in shrapnel turquoise and black,
exiles with a short coat,
a torn pocket, spilling salt, into the truck stop dune,
into the scrub rumble, in the short tin,
getting back,
getting out, the reflected soup,
rope questions
in the ancient marrow, in the bone shoot,

inside the trousers,
this dress with wings, so I curl it, caught

in a blue-redness water bucket, so,
I touch it, inside the territories, occupied,
waiting for *mojo,* inside
the *brujería,* the dance-top falling,
thirteen years old and Egyptian,
soon there's water into a flask, with lips,
with a portrait inside the locket, inside
the captain's engine game,
a tyrant's politeness breathes like this

driving me and you,
through the town alley, with the ass scalded,
a factory whistles in bright steam,

this trembling lamb up the official stairs,
was it compassion, was it my generation, was it
there I cried, where I
opened your hand in mine, where I lost
what I had,
and left it, in fullness and amusement,
at the next century by itself, what

I could not keep, what I could not speak,
what I could not remember, it was you,
it was green and red,

walking up to the mosque, three columns of army jeeps,
in arduous light carrying a young boy, in the jaw, awake

he was in white, with tattoos open
in the name of Abraham, in cuneiform,
for years I was hearing the strings ask me
for a grenade

and the short woman, his mother pressed
with tender knives,
so she could protect herself, they were shrunken
flowers and ashes, a cassette by Parisa
unwinding outside
in the tiny brown tent, the brown watchtowers
in full bloom,
he knew this, this jet weight,
a circular concrete,

when he was grown, it was you,
what I could not remember, was it
Ishmael, or Lucia,
a bit to the left, I left you under the olive tree,
outstretched, a lost code spoiling
from your nightshirt, lime

and rot in Gaza, bloodied, shredded,
where children played by the fountain,
their three fingers pointed,
into darkness, into you,

thirteen years
and the darkness swells down, to their little knees,
to this chair hemorrhaging, in the belly,

newborn in a sack of tear gas
and a pocket hinged
with rocks, the first word in Arabic, this
revolving ocelot clock,

this Jewish Olmec face, in the sliced sun, hidden
microphones, ragged, with the skin of millions, with

a trace of a jade shrapnel, a familiar torture
with the filament, inside the eye, the green into black,
the river-sequined boats, the fire blouse,
in the army night,
there is a bird call, the tiny hands of the iris
in the open road, reaching up,
to the village trumpet,
an old woman in the beggar coat, she is
ready for you,

she is listening with a sweetness, at the center,
a heat from a lagoon in Galicia,
in the shape of my mother,
of your ghost father, without a hat,
a blue coat wing,
this time, out of the boot grave,
out of the wire,

the dim passport from Cairo, the hidden wooden slate,
slashed twice, this sweat justice,
this tombstone ice,

this beat to the riff, reddish, for a petty bureaucrat
collar broken, over the galloping breast, over

the moon saga, in exodus, there we clap
for an amused sail, coming up,
through the potatoes and rifles, the singing mandible,
the lightness of Istanbul and Old Jaffa, the hull
that unwinds, the rust breath from the shirt pocket,
this fever hypnosis, this slash in the leg,

I walk through
the sharpness, this greenish flask in the hoping shoe,

I come to you, now, I bring this,
only for you, what I left behind,
was it the dawn-eyed village alley,
the intrepid nets of hushed camps, you

with your embarcation, gypsy-Indian hair, and me
without a hat, did you love me, walking behind,
mumbling, digging through Palestine, finding myself
in a wooden rice bowl,

in Spanish broken, a carved baglame, upside down,
getting it all, never, they said, never, the tyrants

in flashing suits, I was dead dead
in the fish barrel, in the giant despot cheese wheel,
at the leaning
marketplace, in the tent house,
over you, grayish,
full of rain and lost strings,
and outside, an occupied smell lingers
the rubble office,
two interrogators
with a paper bag of sweet rolls, open,
where we begged, where we saw the waves
behind the olives coming up in razor shapes,

up, over the city,
and the shore full of peasants, my mother carrying
a handsome clock, ticking violins,

the lucid bomb, as in her name, for the mumbling
watchtowers, three columns of army jeeps,
in full dress, our embarcation dripping,
telling the story, studying from the oil lamp
with a sweetness at the center, a jade knot,

an Olmec figurine, clay cast in a shadow,
a briefcase in cuneiform, Egyptian, loud in shrubbery,

shreds, in the tall washer kitchen,
in the hollering closet, in this springtime ankle, tied
to innumerable beings, their hands
clutching ancient discs of sugar and bread
and a wooden spoon, this beggar's Mesopotamia
from the invisible, from

the middle of an unknown forest, beginning with the letters
of an *A* and an *L*, an Arabic *F* and an African *Q*

and a Jewish *M* and a Spanish *H*
and an Egyptian *Z* and a killer's *Z* and
another tyrant's *Z*,
with its beginning pointed and its end pointed,
toward you, toward Istanbul and Old Jaffa,
toward this enigmatic net,

this trouser bag, the torso
out of the spoon, in the braided hair unfolding,
ironically, a tiny scream, reddish,
a pomegranate string-bass beat, another riff
from the open tabla,
all of it, just you and me,
the reflected inspector's coat, the night wing
train wheels to Cairo
and then New York, full of stolen conversations,
a tiny encyclopaedia of stars, over
the embroidered mosque, below the ice stairs,
under the flower vase, this earthen flask,

full of wonderings, the swollen ships,
the healer's touch inside the exiled liquid,
in the secret thigh, in the arm holding you,

it was you,
tattooed to a tear gas sign,
it was me and the open window, without a nurse,
going counterclockwise eating dust
a collection of occupied doorways, after
my own white shadow, the sun in spirals,
on your tattered dress, going into
a perfumed peasant's sword, a laughing insomnia,

innumerable beings, tied to my ankles,
dancing on this asphalt slip, this *cante jondo* train,
whistling through the chasm,

the sweetness at the center, the flannel shirt pocket
made in Lebanon, sewn in Tel Aviv,
with your hand in mine and your face against mine,
again, dance skirts and military caps,
the moon broken and full of amusement, the
stringed air, this frozen patch,
green then red then black, the gleaming coffin,
our continental color gone wild,

a number out of the slave shadows, a number
out of an *L,*

another *L,*
an *L* for last,
very last beggar-worker,
the long long step through the factory yard,
the Southern tent hush, the
crop picker standstill, bread rolls and tobacco

carried secretly through the camps,
in the whipping afternoon, gnashing the engines,
the tractor lifting up the bones of the others, buried
in the sweet sod, with their funny handkerchiefs,

an occupied smell, the hard
cheekbones of dead soldiers, without cloud colors,
and the glance of the singing mother,
still on their tiny heads, wrapped in wetness,
this concrete circle, behind the lost,
hushed numbers without a map for lightness,
the hungry towers stealing my bread,
the love of a woman waving, of a man quivering,
an animal caught in the grasses,

looking up at a crazy star, broken
and upright, going and coming, going and coming,

she wants it said, he wants it said,
soothing, and bluish, reddish, string music and
sweet rolls, behind the stairs,

the passport caught in a foreign bosom, the lagoon in
a boot shape, familiar, it is just desire, they said,
emptiness, fullness, once again, terrible breeze

under the lost door of the petty bureaucrat,
a factory office light bulb,
they feed it and they keep the glistening doorknob,
tight with confessions, they know,
they listen, the strings are going, by themselves,
calling my name, your name hangs
in the cloud air, my father walks alone, again,
and my mother walks next to him,

and she is alone too, and I am here, inside,
with them, it's what you want, it's
in your dress pockets, so much time
through the hourglass, dragging my name,
in cupboard pellets, in the howling silence,
bowing she cannot be seen,

there is something about this, I want to say it,
I want to tell you with words, in kabbala,
the reddish truck

behind the guards, the army opus over you,
cut in half by a jeep, by a masterful stroke
of the driver, learned at night,
the rebel waters peering, taking note,
with skin from our diaries,

I remember all the names,
in cuneiform, the infinite sand walks, dim raceways,
a ship's floor, in the coastal caves,
in the tropical sergeant's cabin, winding,
splintered

a shredded city, rub it,
with prayer and a healer's animal,
a woman with weight calls,
and you will see, with this flask
full of hard coffee, with the Arabic door
and the Hebrew shoe, both banging and burning,
in the moon afternoon sprung open, cast it,

cast it again,
an escapee's spell without a cassock
or an alphabet, the tyrant's silver bites back,
only an open shirt pocket, a sworn word,
to guide you, a golden wheel in promise
across the night train,

the chicken fields full of eyes,
the washer woman wax, the jutting robe of the dead count,

so familiar, a shape concentric, left over,
outstretched in Jerusalem, in something like Kurdish
in a flask, an Egyptian shoe,
for holy walks and night tellings, in wonder,
the village rings,

now, to you, I bring them,
to her, the nameless one with my name, to us, inside,
it took this long, pinned on my forehead,
full of burnished beings, the ones I was given.

THESE

WORDS

ARE

SYNONYMOUS,

NOW

Rodney King, the Black Christ of Los Angeles and All Our White Sins

late April, early May 1992

Listening to Santana, again.
The verdict came down. Four white cops
—found not guilty.

Rodney went down for all of us.
This alley guitar pours its juice into my veins.

His jawbone moved, he spoke
the words of our origin, our names.

The blue-black nightsticks came down
to his plump flesh, across the face, the bones inside.
The bones wavered into the heart
and they exploded for us,

I am kneeling down.

In East Los, La Raza is contemplating Cinco de Mayo
and the French skin that still covers our nakedness.

A cloud with the face of W. B. Du Bois hangs
over the Sherwin Williams paint store

in South Central L.A. —
W. B. said the crises of the twentieth century
would be the color line.

Churn up more blackness through the windows.
Two Chicanas run out of a busted mall, one loaded
with bags of Pampers,
the other with loaves of bread.

Beneath the Harbor Freeway bridge, a tired man
that looks like Ho Chi Minh spits
at the fire trucks going by.

The vapor of kerosene comes up from the apartments
and *chile piquín* peppers on the black asphalt grill.

Streets smell like Guadalajara
where there is a giant crutch being built by the *políticos.*

They are chanting
la tierra mojada —

"The earth has the aroma of rain," they say.
That's what they sing at the mariachi festivals.

This is the *colonia* that blew up a few weeks ago.
Pemex let the gasoline burst underground. Said
it was too expensive to fix the line leaks.

So, they let gas run beneath
the bedroom floors of the Mexicans

—oil and gasoline.

These are the psychic sheets
of our penitence and liberation.

A Harley
—on fire

at the Martin Luther King Boulevard intersection
a few blocks from the Sports Arena. A blonde

woman in jeans—pushed out of her Toyota pickup,
a reddish '84. The Harley is melting

into a chrome praying mantis. Crackle and spit.
Hundreds of oblong bodies rush.

My cousin Vincent
who spent twenty years in the pen sits on his beat-up sofa,
laughs at the blue flash in the corner of his living room.

He picks his nose,
sneers at the newswoman who is beginning
to stumble on the TelePrompTer.

More choppers and tanks.
Tomorrow is paycheck day.

La lana,
la piola,
la rifa,
el cartón,
la feria,

except this time
la gente will cash their welfare checks in a chopper.

Or a National Guard tank,
just maybe.

I am behaving like a Mexican,
the kind you see in Cheech and Chong movies.

The post offices are down
and the banks in San Bernardino are down.

Longo is going up in flames too.
Money is worth a bowl of beans today.

The supermarkets are open, everything is free.
Ginsberg was wrong about the supermarket

—Whitman
and Lorca are elsewhere.

This is my atonement,
this is my resurrection,
this is the way of the black cross,
the brown crown of thorns.

The liquor stores are ours. The laundries are ours.
Shirts we never wore are finally pressed, ready
for church, and the toasters
with extra-wide slots are ours too.

There is a pearl-white Mercedes being kicked in
by six kids with Adidas and torn faces.

A bloodied Chicano is taking pot shots
at my neighbor, Taiji, as he swerves
into an on-ramp going west. The Guard
is on the way, the *federales* are on the way.

A cop shoots mace into a white boy's eyes
—how does it feel, how does it?

Another guy fondles his own breasts
as he looks at a VCR behind the window.
A pack of Michelob,
a gold suit and a helmet,
badges

and justice
and ratchets.

Sirens come for Rodney's spirit. Someone gets run over,
the legs are crushed on Normandie Avenue—

a young vato's brains slide down
the headrest of his '59 Biscayne;

on the way back from a soccer game
he met a bullet with his name.

Rodney has answered all the silences.
It is a tender voice, a cavernous tenderness.

Greenish smoke curls toward Hollywood Boulevard
Edward James Olmos comes out to clean up with brooms.

There is a crew of white students
huddled in a hamburger diner called Burgertime,
they are saying—

Blacks and minorities got their share already
"Why are they doing this?"

"Why?" they say,

and another newscaster uses the word *animal*
as he peeks through the tube.

and Rodney's white lawyer's face stretches
as he becomes black in an uncanny way.
He is looking for more words about justice.

There is no Black Christ.

I said it to get myself going. I was loaded
with stupor and complacency. Because
I live in the suburbs of North Fresno.
Because I see fat tractors and rigs

smooth the ground
for more cells of silence.

Now, I have spilled my guts
in a Mexican way.

Need more fuel now;
thought I was clean. Thought I could do

with the other things,
but I need the fuel now, need the cheap kind.

My wife Margarita is upstairs taking a shower.
The water is churning through the ceiling
making high-pitched sounds,
shredding sounds.

More smoke. Another line of dead,

nameless dead with one name for all of them.
Maybe our name, maybe

it is my name and your name they are calling.
An old woman in an oversized sweater,
in denims, drinks
a hot Gatorade from the mess of a 7-Eleven.
A Korean vato and a Mexican dude
are fingering their mouths

—their stores are in ashes. These are the ashes.
Cross your foreheads on this Ash Friday,

this Ash Saturday of black palms
and talkative gutters full of rainbow juice,
the kind that comes from radiators, skulls,
cracked batteries.

This year we had a long Easter.
It got caught up in a bad cycle of drought,
earthquakes, blood, glue,
and pregnant cats and bird nests thrown open
by a car crash.
The broken birds are soapy without skin,

there is a tiny purple ball still
ticking inside their stomachs;

the beaks are too yellow
—the color of emergency plastic tape,
the type cops put around a murder scene.
Don't step on them, if there is anything you do
—please don't step on them.

At Union Square, in San Francisco,
they are ripping down the neon signs,
right across from the St. Francis Hotel. My mother
worked there as a salad girl in the forties,
right after the war;

that's when Lawrence Welk was the main feature
on weekends, and they are on Market Street too
by the Embassy Theater
where you can see a porno show for one dollar.

I am carrying a triple landscape in my head.
Walking around with tears on my ragged face.
Congas and timbales by the trashcans.

I can see everything—San Francisco,
Guadalajara, and the city which was an empire
once upon a time. I used to go there
as a kid and look at my hands to make sure
I was there—
to remember myself there
by the shape of my hands.

This is the way of the Gods in the Streets,
this is the Gospel of Rodney King,
the Black and Brown Wand of Inspiration.

City Paint

Reddish flared patches cover our soft houses, our streets.
A wanton perfume seems to pour, thicken these summery decks.
I play cards with a stranger. I pick at secret sentiments. I spin
little pictures for the heart—at anyone's gestured request.

The businessman going north is my guest or I am
asked by others in less formal attire. (I know this—
their ill-freedom gives them away.) A young sailor smokes
a cigarette, a sailor with the lips chafed, chalk marked.

Too much desire, I tell him. The military are marching
as ever. I take stock of these frayed moments. I think
as a clown; the shadowy Mexican kind, leaning jagged
in marketplace air, believing his purplish sparrow puppet.

I linger with an ache, always. Still, I laugh, axe shaped
inside, a Jack of resentments—raised from a trailer
where I was born. Things give me away: my uncle's death—
uncle Geno who cared for my mother as a child. Pure color.

The colors pull me. Somber green blueness. But everyone
stays lithe, somehow. Jugglers of the boulevard, powdered.
We never talk about this, this age. Costumes, disguises.
The evils of the frozen glance stop me, hold me again.

I sit on the park benches. I listen. People look this way;
the left side of the face, darkened. The left angle
of their little rooms falling—one side of the bed pushing
away from their spotted bodies. This is what stops me.

I relax. Stroll into the used bookstores. Astutely
they notice the sections I walk in: Adolescent Literature,
Life magazines cut with thin blue razors. This is how I live
taking note of temperatures, plump forearms loosening.

I'll tell you where I live. An off-white bridge sprayed
with lovers' frenzies leads to my cottage. Under the dull
shield of cement—rafters rattle—men and women hunched,
sitting on their roped boxes. I know this gallery too; gold

leaf torsos glazed in Renaissance promise. Everyone here
gambles on this river shore, goes up the moss mounds
into town, carries a fish pail—waits in line for loaves, aces.
You turn an ivy gate. For a while you talk to the barber

about your little girl and then you mention the curative
powers of the ocean. It is best to gather it in a house jar,
my father used to say. Drink it and it will heal you. Outside
my front window the amber stumps groan; how copper

strips and blurs across these flat planes of the factories.
I read these signs every day. I keep them in my sketch book.
Sometimes I fold them in my pockets. I tap my fingers
there. Let me tell you more about this city. The Victorian

houses are opaque, religious, swollen spires. It is
in the kitchens where people sleep. I never see anyone
walk out or gaze up to lift a windowpane. The second
floor is too weak now. A white shroud covers the stairs.

The shroud falls on the streets too. It seems to comfort
their souls; everyone rests this way, huddled by their
bright yellow stoves. Fire spokes twist as so many years
in the boiling clocks. Then, the docks; hazel, ancient piers;

bitten shore lamps, hollow singing boats, strafed stones,
violet smoke. The muffled music in the reefs calls me.
People pass by—they name me John. They cross their arms
at the rails remembering their crumbled countries;

the parchment map they followed, rust knives they met.
I see them praying for open sable woods, drinking from
the baroque fountains, whispering to lost ones, telling
their grown sons to forgive them, to write soon. I play.

I toss kings from a distance. Sometimes I bring my
ribboned guitar and sing Mexican riddles. Tell of Plácido,
the crazy man who collected brooms so he could build
a ladder to the sky. In other quarters I am a rogue dancer.

Hotels are my favorite theaters. I sway my long tattered
dinner coat, I make people laugh. My red cap shaped as
a canoe; amuse them—the olive fragrance, a burst of memory
makes them see other things: a man with his black gloves

his lover's letter upstairs in the vestibule. Look at him
smile. I pirouette with Gerard the headwaiter, Carla
the hostess with chocolates—her puffed white legs. Then
we laugh again, nibble. No one points to the resolute

woman about to sever her romance—coffee and penitence,
she says. He says, sugar, two please. I've kept all this
in my journals. Napkins are perfect artifacts. They are left
in flight or ecstasy. I weigh them for signs, for lives.

I stalk the square. I snap blisters, the ochre finish
of abandoned storefront walls. You can scale old rooftops,
feel the braille of end pipes jutting, or archways where
water collects on pebbled ceilings. There is heat, steam.

Below—the library, hot, caged; so still with a woman
inspired. Her pencil elegant, feverish. Husbands thumb
the newspapers, too quickly. Their wives remember them
talking, a curl in their eyes. Desire again, a mark of rage.

With one or two fingers they unravel the well-sewn locks
of their brilliant hair. Nights; I find men confessing in game
parlors; no crucifix. A Caravaggio, drunk by the coin machine
just revolves, pulls his stained, solemn collar. Tomorrow

at the porch; the knees will fold in consolations. Look
across the lawn to the perfect greenness. Daytime
bathes their knuckles; a family album opens. Hands rise
slowly to cup the mouth—a picture is measured, adored.

A few newcomers circle the downtown alleys and arcades
where old beggars with large coat pockets and the young
ones with soft hands sit back on tin gallons, a chipped fire
hydrant. A tiny comedian puffs from the makeshift stage.

Open cream jars on patio chairs, drinks. A whipping taxi
changes gears; a rouge scarf. The knitted stars of a night lamp
spill on the stoic curb. With the late evening radio I hum
over my wedge-table, tap royal faces under the filtered light.

These Words Are Synonymous, Now

for Robert

On the way to school I tell my son
remember to read—read fast. At every curb
think of three things, examine the faces
the eyes—especially the eyes, be quick.

The other day I picked up an old paperback
Houdini, the Handcuff King who slipped off
Scotland Yard's shackles in minutes.

Holding the book in my left hand, I churn it
with the fleshy mound of my palm my thumb
makes small circles on the cover.
These words are synonymous now:

University
Steel

Light
Nothing

Poets
Rags

Words
Paper

I am working on a play—the world in twenty years.
There is a sentry, a clown and a warrior; a slave colony
on the verge of escape from the video eye. The eye
sees everything. Picture the slender man in the supermarket
holding up a small can of cranberry sauce—weighing
the contents he is concerned with a stamp-size
inscription. Ingredients:

sodium, fructose,
pectin, artificial flavoring.

Tomorrow his daughter will bleed from the mouth;
the blood will glisten hot, wavy—her tall boyfriend drinks.
She runs to him; he traps her when daddy sleeps.
There are too many recorded tragedies. No one listens.
Listen to the little bronze gears inside the computer;
everyone owns one, delivers upon the keys. Listen again:

the *A*
the *Z*
the Asterisk
slapping, so quiet
mournful, so pious.

Treacheries
Falsehoods

Big words. My friends are afraid to speak them.
The television offers brilliant young men,
immense shoulder braces tumbling across the green,
a pigskin against the solar plexus, a broken leg
juts out wanting to kick the audience, sweltering,
saliva on shirts, ribbons, cold bottle Pepsies.
I work toward good things, play inexpensive games—
a miniature clay house with two black windows,
pearled marbles with yellowish zigzag lines,
a funny thumb size, plastic, German luger pistol.
I surprise myself. I finally figured people out.

The Rhyme-Master, Elder King of Ink
who bequeaths Grace upon the Speechless.

The Child-Molester who receives tribute
from his political colleagues.

The Daughter-Monkey caged by her own aging mother
who will never talk to another man again.

I think of my mother. Tiny ancient—who saved broken birds
from the sidewalk rubbing their heads with herbs, who
waited nineteen years for me to return. I never did.
I read about the thalamus, the intricate web of the brain.
My friends use these words too:

Literary Production
Feminist Art
Ideology—the Underclass

while our little mothers shrink,
die without us. We never say Sacrifice. It smells of religion.
My Aunt Lela is caught in a second story above a ham-and-eggs
diner. She's eighty-four—when she walks she falls
on the cement every time her legs give out.
I tell her use a cane like my mother did.

People don't like to hear this, they say poetry must have
a fancy curl in the center—don't complain, they say. I ask them
do you have better figures?

In the United States
the per capita income is $27,000 a year
in Malawi Africa it's $160 in Nayarit Mexico up
on Indian land—a bowl of corn squash and seeds.

I sit at the library, gaze across the table; trees, windows
are continuous; the telephone post connects with the leaves
darkness crawls up the bark, tears daylight to pieces.
These are labels and empty synonyms:

Poetry and chalk dust
Horror and humanity
Laughter and spit

I tell my son—that's good, learn the cello, listen to its womb,
take your time, take your time.

ON THE
DAY OF THE
DEAD,
MR. EMPTINESS
SINGS OF LOVE

Norteamérica, I Am Your Scar

Get out of my walled infinity
of the star circle round my heart.
                    Vasko Popa

My friends grab at their shoulders
at odd times. So do I.

There is something eating at the ligaments.

We crouch as if in a snow blizzard.
A stranger's blue wool weighs on us.

And somehow, we still lift
our delicate fingers;
a true gentleness moves.

Our portraits hang on the precipice.

A crazy quill left
for an old woman's barbed hook
undulates inside the small of our back.

It is hard to walk, like this.

It makes us sullen, silent,
with rough lips dying from madness but,
then, our hair that refuses to stop growing
pounds its black tubing into the sea,

excavating
making room for a forest or
a desert of terrible ink.

And there we sing, at last;
a fang with lightning;

a half-sun breaking from the second story of a tidal wave;
this unfinished stone fist novel unraveling all its wetness.

A quarry knife
I carry, for you. You take it now.
It grows slowly,
inside, an echoing razor, flutelike in a Midwest bar

in Davenport called El Charro,
or Lee Choy's or Fry's Grill on Dubuque Street.

But, you don't see this,
you say you are campaigning.
I received the champagne bottle and the bow tie.

You said everything is ready
and that everyone, even Alma Guttenberger,
the librarian at Haines Hall,
will finally see the color green, beginning emerald.

Here, you say,
take it:

a green saxophone, a scream leashed,
held against our chest.

Inhale
exhale.

And see how our undershirts, our poor fishing skirts tear
and the trouser pocket shoots a wishbone, a toothpick, something
that we've kept for ourselves.

You see, this is what we have;
all we have. You know this.

Your hand bleeds, and the blood smashes onto our roofs
like a reconnaissance map. Or is it our bile?

We are so tied to you. Our hind leg
limps with the cadence of all your daylight thefts
when you leave our yards
with our small icebox under your arm.

We know how you have taken our fender.
How you have lured our dishrag.
How you have hammered
our almond-eyed typewriter ribbon.
We see how you polish your claws.

This is my village, full of crosses, swollen, dedicated to your industry
groomed in your spirit of bank flowers and helicopter prowls.

I want to say good-bye Big Man.
I want to say farewell Holy Jaw.

But you see, there is very little left to do, now,
except go to the park and relax with you; take your hand
in the shape of my hand

and point with the powdery grace of night,
point to the phosphor crescent on your palm, this scar
you say you got from hunting wild game

somewhere in the South, when you used to dream
above saguaro and when you towered over
the wire coils across the endless borders
and military bridges into my anguish,
into my resentments.

I point there because you will find me
in a shape so familiar, so close to you;

in your language, in your chequered English neckties,
in your translucence and your innumerable notes of ash
and penitence; I point there, you

strong man with a sanguine palm tree leaf
jutting from the robes you wear. The ones we make
with our daily smoke of washerwoman wax.

Listen to me.
Your scar speaks to you.

Your dreams know the scar very well,
there, the scar lives with its bulbous velvet root on fire.
Let's walk together, in this light.

Tonight there will be an animal fair
somewhere in this curled-up nation.
Look there.

This is the age of the half-men
and the half-women.

I say to you, now, I celebrate
when we shall walk with two legs once again
and when our hands shall burst from your hands.

Fuselage Installation

(My loved ones drift into nothingness
—with little red gifts still
in their anxious arms. Little shirts.)

Blaze, the missile shards; your fuselage glitter, stuttered
over the wild crazed mountains; a blast at the exact interval
when coffee was being served. On the last plate,
a frayed napkin casts a claw shadow.

Lift. The hill with little people—tardy saints. Kneel.
They are your lecturers, your gloomed witnesses
with elongated hats; alarming
scarves blossom from their torsos.

The fuselage is—the child, her back mandril blue.
What stone amphitheater sings, what peasant trumpets glare for her?
This dragon vestment is all we have, now: nameless quills,
unknown fins, burning gauze without candlewicks.

You assemble new artillery, set up a helmet monument
inevitably, you salute with pleasure. We follow
in this dome—your basilica of quiet blood. This is your kingdom,
earthquake light.

Penance? Go there
to the waters of the glazed city. All the electric fish, whitened,
loosened from their tarnished silver boots—the ones they used
to bully you.

They too float above your hand, eerie
their purple smoke mouths, triumphant.

Writing by the Hand

According to the pen, the writer was sitting
in an office space—a dense cube. Air and light;
shredding thoughts, the tiny darkened scarf
jutting out from the fingertips. An indigo.
Of course, it wasn't a scarf. As I opened
the fountain—my tongue reached the opaque
film in language. Chain. Coagulation. A call
came in from behind, an attempt to give
selfless love—only the spirit bestows it;
waves from the spirit-light as it bounces
out from the shirt. Then, the desk flipping
an ace of diamonds from the thumb: a reason,
one more milliliter of longing—a baby wink
for Mother Jasmine. The pen was taciturn
yet, busy, very busy stabbing the rubbery mat
under the arm; this soft sponge plenum.
You have to admit that this is ridiculous,
Pedro Towers thought as he pressed on;
the fountain was very busy. Pedro was staring

at the little snarls of indigo leaves. Who
was Mother Jasmine? Does she have the maps
to the fountain? Is she a fictitious card figure?
Why is this pen blending so well into the film?
Can the bluish waters lead to other tables
beyond language? Unassembled, crying. Still.
Laughing out loud? A mischievous Dante in New
York, for example. The arm so fastened. Elbows,
so devout. Every follicle on the epithelium bends,
sways again. In some uncanny way, things
are going awry; the fountain suggests this.
Pedro wishes to celebrate in a particular zone.
Away with brain-shadows, he says. No more.
Pedro, a man about town, about country, feels
(yes, feels) that everything is false, now.
This blackish mat hiding under the wrists; this
is disappearing, he says. A nothing-blue.
Lies. Below him. He must try to capture
what happened earlier—according to the box
in the room. There is a germ nosing up:
his will, of course; memories, potentials,
dances—signs left on this side. Not enough
for the pen to go down. In the end, Pedro
Towers must contract a fever—a Paradiso
shell glowing within the shirt pocket.
Timeless. Whatever articulations he invents
will be yours. Myth and coffee, Jasmine or milk.

AIDS Hearing in the Metropolis

Instead, not one word comes from your parched lips,
and that passing crowd naively believes that you and
your executioners are out for a stroll.

Solzhenitsyn

A carafe of white wine glistens. Onyx table;
engraved glasses. You stammer.

You cannot imagine yourself here—the little cushions.
Phrasing; a measured sneer. Coils.
You, he says. Just *you.*

The spirit of deception is evident—a Goya
on the north wall; an ancient persecution

gives them away; their tempered steps,
dry desert branch flowers in a period vase.

There are no luxuries in the deeper quarters.
Not one. All this could occur in a familiar suburb:
Lincoln Hills, Silver Strand.

Honorable lapels;
slippery gloves to plague you—a quarantine
in the fold of every signal; you can sense it.

The maneuver: a progress report will play back
on the spindle machine; motifs of kindness to baffle you.

The interrogators will feign surprise
(wise boys). You will even be allowed
to depart from the usual trappings of recent detentions.

You won't notice the soft-spoken man's sabotage
(a disease) color the knitted conversation:

Syringe—transfusion, incubation sheath,
where, how did you spread it, how often
did you follow our instructions?

The splatter leaf; cinnamon dark,
there, your skin, oblong wounds behind the calf.
Proof. Just *you.*

You will look up, again. This time, a makeshift clinic
—the room, experimental. Graphic sideboards, X rays
a white knot in the lung.

The assistant strokes his little blue chin.
Humidity, the hand-held meters, straps.
Straps? You say.

You are wearing summer attire, light cottons.
They want a quaint stitching of folklore to comfort you.
So, they tell you

in your country everyone dances inside
a sand circle, on a precipice. Oracular moons.
Kill a regal bull for solar blood,

rattle deer horns. Listen to his baritone song;
a village seer at the horizon; only he can heal you
at no cost to the soul. They taunt you.

You are forbidden to call the city officer.
The camera switch clicks. Zoom: their empire
eliminator virus on the screen.

Everyone is so hospitable;
you can't believe the film, the intentions.
The studio executive peers into your eye.

He examines—a fertile track, the findings;
double codes, new spores; spirals gone awry.

You sense the wild mantis
glaring into your windows;
yellow tin spikes in the grasslands.

To turn back,
only if you could. Time. Time. Time.

You want your cigarette, your withered arm to come
up for recognition. How many years, now—in this office,
in this octagon city cell?

You were summoned here from an elegant sedan.
You were going home from the gym. Lisha, your bright wife,
who thinks of you here?

Play your thin knife fingers, you;
your tiny nervous harps; there is still breath
in the veined mask—speak. Or point. Point.

The Soldier's Bluish Mane

I want to ask you. Can you touch
the snowy light mask above me?

A bluish mane
—my soft neck. Speak, for once. Summer
flays me as it will flay you,
spin inside, spin,

and sing to me—simple lines:
More daylight now, more reddish light—
tiny leaves burn.

I will call for a tree-hunger; limbs
to push on, nibble, lift up. Wise bird faces,
give me your spiked cashmere hats. Hurry,

ride this fourth-ring floor, this convex room.
And my son, you must tell me, where is he?
Too many walk into my dreams, now.

Who will carry my nightcoat? What visitor
with a porcelain cup, sweet bread rolls?

This halo fire. This evening, one more veiling
one final hand-knit sweater. Gaunt ultramarine
to watch me.

My favorite one
you used to wear it, when you visited me
held my glistening hair at noon. Floating.

A pastel window appears more often,
by the supply room, above the rubbish tin.
It fools me, it mocks me. Near my bed,

torturers dance their charities; all in a Styrofoam cup.
A couplet of evil candies—to lift my hand again.

To turn my eyes up again; a salamander in my girlish mouth,
peeks, grumbles; his black spot tongue, hesitant.

I will rise somewhere, at midnight, I pray
in my quiet fright kitchen with a meal for my son,
the glaring plate in his hand, a shiver

in his spine. But, for now, I hum, nestled
in foreign nurse arms.

A pastor wants to console me.
I say hopscotch. My little mirror is best. Do you know
how to Charleston? My half-sister never danced.

I can see her, arriving, now: a terrible knot inside her
well-pressed blouse, a lost coin muffled in a thick pocket.
Water, please. Water, then.

Glamorous Treacheries

A tiny jet
plows into the field and there, all we can distinguish
is a colonel's cap—rustling, under the torn fleece of a sycamore.
I think of a human being—

how he becomes quasi-political, forges
his afternoon leave time inadequately.

A young officer hardens, turns to a small book:
Glamorous Treacheries—prefers the diffuse tragedies,
the little ones that stick.

The process of subversion carries weight,
I know. What do their spouses have to say? It is in the news,
almost on a daily basis.

All this conjures up an uncanny set of images: spectacles in a lake,
frozen, parchment maps with the *E*'s cut out. They want something
more baroque in our lives.

We want thoroughness, a bridge to be built
at every inconsistency. Our friends say

we need to rethink all the obstructions to ourselves.
A list appears;
keywords: *precision, alchemy, trial.* It is no use,
you say. So, then we pretend guilt in the purse, impossible sins.

We begin to hammer at a balsa chamber behind the pillow.
Write a novel: peaches, toast—a boy, Orion, his past lives.

Eavesdrop, again
and again. A goatskin, a propeller in the air.
The years, we say. Flights to another kingdom.

The Sea During Springtime

I go to sleep on one beach.
Wake up on another.
           Raymond Carver

Come down to this stoney day
—an evening when I lift my head.

Gaze at the architecture,
greenish, sealed.

Peasant shadows and hours pour from my skin.
It isn't a burial mound I am looking at.

It is lost beneath the lead and wood
and the angles of my pressing mouth.

I cannot drink from its tides.
It is a sea that will open in another sky.

There is only a white tiger
pacing beneath the black.

Designs inside my bones.
Aurelia Quintana is dead.

Laundry faith woman, solitary soup overseer
in an oven for holy brooms.

I circle her from a distance
in el Valle de San Joaquín.

My uncle lifts her from a candlelike bench
shaped by silence and his captive soul.

My aunt smells of plants tonight—lavish,
thick lipped, wet, spinning in the jade center.

More shadows, embossed,
carved with my solemn left hand.

The burnisher that I keep is well defined and alive.
I earn this knife from dirt and apartment lamps.

I earn the kerosene and accordion smoke.
Once my mother hid there while she was kissing.

Once I wept there and saw my father leave.
He was leaving the same way we left every city.

Now my spirit pushes me toward the tower.
No one is there—except my grandfather, Alejo.

He is the man who cut maguey,
pulled the whitish juice from a pointed heart.

He is the worker who turned to salt. Pulque
down the arms. A tiny soul slobbering birth.

I am carrying the dead. I can hear them
nibble my ears with their faint tongues.

Late hours—a spirit sits on my head.
Then it throws my legs to one side.

I raise my hand and grab the night air,
silvery in its grain.

Silvery in its oceans. Silvery
in its feminine voices.

You never visited.
You walked the streams.

When you told me, singing
I saw your dead child.

He was locked away, beneath
Briars and merciless woods.

After he fell,
No one looked for him.

And now?
And now?

The waters are yellow and blue by the trail,
reflecting the oval sky.

A boat rushes with women, men and children.
Dark hair and swaying torsos.

An old man with a reddish beard stands
alone by the sails, laughing.

He asks me to cross this bluish bridge
where people lean over and gaze.

A watercolor of green and shredded violet
comes to light my face again.

There are gulls in the air. A black hat.
Carnations, crescent disks. Prayer.

A little battle for heat. Naked
without a jacket, greyish. I give thanks.

My belly is deep into the sod. A baby boy
in cottons and a pomegranate flush calls me too.

Three steps above me. Two roses above his head,
bowed. He is also a wheel of concentric infinites.

I can place my tears on his round arms.
I can place my death on his shoulders.

Above the ground, in my stupor
—this is the way I walk.

A black pagoda comes up through the waves.
I am full of beginnings. I am full of wonderings.

String music. Mussels and sea bark.
Clams as flint and pursed as castanets.

An open palm inside. Aurelia leans
by the grasses. Her legs cross the sands.

Aurelia pulls at her rings and shawls,
soft and earthen. We dance in a full circle.

Around the coral. She steps into a wider ring.
Water washes my feet, goes up into my navel.

Another wave thrashes the satin arm of my spirit.
I am ready to sing. My aunt Aurelia weeps.

Aurelia sits on a parchment—
the one my mother carried since she was a girl.

It is made of fibers and leaves gathered on the way.
She is young. She is restless and slides down a rock.

Her hair long—going. Snow and sunlight
in the winds. It is springtime.

It must be springtime in the mountains
where the sea begins.

Auburn

Your auburn hair
over my fingers—runs away.

A ribboned shore, designs awake
by strange mountians.

You look up. Frayed omens,
reddened clouds, infinite systems.

I know of a stream.
Sway me in its olive smoke.

Lift the curled leaves—
a pebbled shawl for its tiny trees.

Bring me your careful notebooks.
Boyhood calligrams. Remember

when we found a yellow-green
pinecone and you said it was the earth
with a spike shoe, a spike dress?
Slip away from the marbled cliff.

You
with a raging spiral heart.

Aviary

You were on a square, moving toward a bus,
a flowery jacket across the arms. Curvatures, kisses
hidden in a volume of wires.

This was significant
—your extended hands, shirt pocket leaning, waiting.
I was outside too, loose, full with free affection. A feverish journey
at our touch. All this. As always

every olive cloak wanting to tear from the clouds—all writers
in America wanting the hazel lights inside their asylum(s):

a spirit engine speaking
the timepiece face on their wrist.

Dull brooch, I says.
Dull brooch lost under the sidewalk rail.

Why have I found it so neatly,
quietly folded, resilient?

Pedro Towers, is that you again? Looking
for certainties. Begin again — the arms first
then the fingers.

Feel the other strange fingers on the same hand.
That is all.

Pick up the gypsy lock, the letters beyond the body,
the night writings. A taciturn breeze, a brilliant
pass through the signs curled in the old cities (yes, walk signs).

The avenue waving, the lovers high up,
about to embrace.

Iowa Blues Bar Spiritual

Little Tokyo bar—

ladies night, smoky gauze balcony, whispering. Tommy Becker,
makes up words to "La Bamba"—request by Hard Jackson,

mechanic on the left side of Paulie, oldies dancer, glowing
with everything inside of her, shattered remembrances, healed

in lavender nail polish, the jagged fingernail tapping. So
play it hard above this floor, this velvet desert. I want

the Titian ochre yeast of winter, keyboard man, fix your eyes
on my eyes and tell me, handsome, how long will I live?

How many double-fisted desires, crushed letters, will I lift
in this terrain? And this rumbling sleeve, this ironed flint

of inquisitions and imaginary executors, where shall I strike,
what proud stones? Will this fauna open for me, ever, this fuzz,

anointed beak inside the bartender's mirrors, etched doves,
a cautious spiral Harley tank, hissing, this Indian bead choker on Rita's neck?

How long shall we remain as wavy reflections,
imitators of our own jacket's frown? Who shall awaken first?

Margo Fitzer, the waitress? I will say, Queen Margo, sing to me
stoic princess of slavering hearts, three faint lines creased

on your satin belly, toss our planet onto your umber lacquer tray,
too empty now; make the earth spin its dog rhapsody, erotic

through this silvery off-ramp and flake, unfurl. We tumble across
this raceway in honey-glazed traces, our arms ahead, the hands

flying to Ricky's Ice Cream Parlour, outside. I want to own one
someday, maybe on Thirty-Second Street. You will see me

in my gelled waved hair, my busy wrists—so fast, a clown's
resolute gloves, dipping faster than finger painting—except

I'd be stirring milk and the chocolate foam of love, churning,
burning this sweet spirit, more uncertain, than the celestial

sheaths above the prairie frost. See the boy coming, they chide,
leaning, how he crosses his legs, his eyes dreaming, sideburns

just shaved clean. He weighs the sour slate on his father's breath;
perfume, fortune, cards left on the bleeding table. Milo Wilkens, drummer

at the curve, strokes his nipples with his arms as he hits the high hat.
Somewhere in the back rooms, I know, a shrine, orange sponge cushions,

two toilets and a wire wound wicker box, to leave flowers, occasional
offerings by the Johnson County dudes, detasslers in jersey ties.

Talk no more, enjoy. Darling singer, let your starry blouse sway me,
steal this fresh peach half from its amber juice; I want the moon

in this nectar, too. The flashing cymbals, feverish. Who can strike
a votive candle, love, or sleep in this electronic night? Just listen

to the two-part harmony, laughter, peeling beyond the cemetery, beyond
the Iowa river—where the spike hat rooster bristles his tiny ears,

bows his head, and sips from the dark cannister under the carved pearl-stone.
And then, returns. Let us drink, salute the bright spokes of meal, the dying

wands of river blossoms, grandmother's sacred hair; listen, her soprano
owl, her bluish melody, so thin. Another glass please, we shall dance

once again, our eyebrows smearing against each other's cheekbones, loud
with a Midwest sweat, a cantata from the crosshatch amp, click it.

Click it, for wild kind rain, forgiving seasons, for the blushed bread
of our shoulders and thighs, this night, everyone is here. Even Jeff Yoder

came all the way from Illinois, to fill a bucket with passion, ruffled,
thick. O sax player with a jail needle tattoo, leap onto this wet pavement,

call my lonesome tempest heart, its buried mother's kiss, bless us
in staccato, with quivers of oak branch greenness, and sparrow longings

riff over this brutal sky, give us your bell filled, conjure your tropic,
our lover's breath. Blues bar dancers, jangling gold popcorn, chord makers,

opal-eyed Suzie in a flannel shirt; we beckon the spark, the flaring
this lost body to live.

Alligator

On the alligator's back
viola tenderness, dark diamond

roses.
Pedro Towers sleeps.

Concrete palisade, blue mystery
his rough tears;

wine to drink. I walk
up to the furniture market, oblong
liver,

madness bloated—the steeple.

In my hurried coat, in parsley night print—
green phosphor

lamps, the heavens
must part. Without love?

The gaunt clock, kabbala—ticking.
At what hours, brothers,

O sisters,
can you tell me?

At the Town Pump on 16th,
the speckled wino's fist
burns without

a wise thumb—lost
on a basketball bet.
Smoke draped,

etched, hardened; luster
of garlic robust whiteness,

bleached face. I go.
I want to bring my father home
now. Clarinet

voice, long coat. Blessed naked leaves
in his pocket. Sing

for his blue coat wing.
Who

will bake bread now, caress
ferns, drag forward the dust at the gate?

Alligator
Alligator eat

my tiny tree heart, ringed
rugola, rugola.

I will grow stronger. Taste
the yellowed herbs, your wild
eyes. I will strike

these dwellings—convex cushions,
shiny toy chests: drops, academies.

Towers Lake thickens; stillness.
fury. He sleeps now
wet—a handkerchief, the forest

symphony.
He dreams the crumbled recipe,

tangled—sweet:
Apples, raisins
cinnamon,

lightning—an embarkation, spice.
Rest a little, rest now, you

rise again.

Blue Coat, White Shirt

for my father, Felipe Emilio, in memory

You had come back from the chalk blue hospital
your left leg as supple as your right. Where
is your wheelchair?

Where is that two-by-four you bought
when Mama wheeled you to the hardware store?

Remember how you wanted to build a foot,
a leg without gangrene?

Leg fresh as pine
to take you up "C" Street, to Broadway,
talk with Mr. Kelly, the Irishman
or the policeman who asked,

when did you get out of jail?
And you answered the day *you* got in.

You were always hammering the air,
the wood seed, a pearl of breath inside the plank.

Unexpected knots. Tender seams. Shadowy nails
for a house. A scrap of earth, an axle to carry us home.

Busy, so busy in my dream.
I could not turn, look at my feet, your shoes.

Hear the leather heel move,
so slightly into the ground.

Sand circles
lost around our house; every turn,
connecting the lamppost, a snapping curb,
an escape ladder.

The harmonica you left,
I lost.

My mother remembered you.
She must be with you now.

Both of you
in her old apartment. Third floor
above the piano repair.

Every morning, I reach for her
with a candle, a wintry match.

I never took the time to look
at my hands on your arms.

The thin hair in heat
weaves and roams—
shoos me
to this half-lit doorstep.

You were under a tree. I had seen you earlier,
I wasn't sure; you?

I was clutching my philosophy books,
pushing through the week. Like the others,
I don't pick up leaflets—I just go

up the hill
through my hollow-eyed calendar.

A blue coat.

We were in Grapeday Park, Escondido.
You stroke the grass, I stare at the gnarled heart
of an old willow. A fifty-cent piece

rolled in my cuffs. My front teeth loose,
an apple in your coat pocket.

Did I run from the shivering hospital?
Was I darkening under the low ceiling
at the foot of your chromed wheels?

Am I awake or am I sleeping
on my yellowed notebooks, my face blurring?
Is a young boy falling in the distance,

are the leaves unraveling their tears?

This is the carpenter's son, dressed in straw
—the hammer writer.

This is his raging shoulder.
Here is the flaring of the pine veins.

I walk bent
to your loosened steps, this
anxious stream.

Where is the hammer you left me
will I need it tomorrow?

Under this tree
by the ice light
a leaf opens its star-shaped coat, into the air,
spins—your white shirt.

Loss, Revival, and Retributions
(Neon Desert Collage)

I've been bad-mouthing love too much
—chipped white in sadness; the solar collar

above me; an onyx flame. I am running,
smashing my Dodge over relief maps.

There's a peering scarf ahead, maybe Andalusian—
a Ziegfeld dancer with a tender belly? I sing: Rise.

I command her: Rise! Too many roulettes haunt me;
there is a catch in the black and red velvet air.

Nothing left,

but to reach for the pinball-soul inside. Swagger,
stay there—(please stay there) for once. A chrome

pearl speaks in southern Spanish accents. A Moorish boot
swings out: my new master—in oxblood. In chalk dust.

Infinity burns on my tongue.
If only I could spit again, bruise the wastelands;

a polychromatic insignia from this gut vest—to please.
I am not like that anymore. O square-shouldered guitars,

pop me another drink. An off-beat hooligan flamenco
slaps my back—the wind. Bring me fortune, I say—

fortune again—a shredded red star—on the inside
of my knee; my mother's tiny prophecies.

I believe in the Goddess of Oasis and Velocity,
her ragged sky skirt to pull me. My last destination.

There is elegance—a glassy palm tree sparkles ahead.
A starry fruit, bluish hands, waiting. Desire. Or is it electricity?

I am coming up fast without water. The number 27, someone
stands there, with orchids. I can see it all, now. Above
the wild lonely palms.

On the Day of the Dead,
Mr. Emptiness Sings of Love

Maga plays at the blue tarp—the tavern spilling its melancholy letters,
its worker's glove. So, a little boy stops for a millisecond, a whisper, inside
the flannel, his fawn, his new eye. Twenty years trembling with a cane, twenty

carcass freights sold to the executive with a big hand. It is all in the books, up
there, see? Up there, the stairs, go—Mr. Emptiness is shredding lettuce, in
a Portuguese accent, in the wee hours of the Souls on the Day of the Dead.

He sings of love. All of us, he says—only, if only we have if's and so's, that is
all we will need to leave the archipelago, the moss, the captain's rock, leave
a wide-brimmed hat, a circuit of factories, garment-makers, necessary tortures.

There is deepness in the piano at Maga's bar—she says it comes from
strings that lead down, in staccato. A little man weeps at the crazy steel foot—
his beloved architecture, again. I want to smell the Mexican air, ribboned

in petroleum, afloat in fancy orphan scrawl, this is how I survive, he says,
carrying these charts and their tilted ghosts after earthquake light; twenty
years—each woman pays at the Mount, each man lifts at the banquet. Twenty

prayers in a thimble-razor. The cargo for the hangman is rage, simply—rage
and salt in a briefcase, a half-flask of seawater at the desk. And he will never
reach it. His glove is about to peel; his sacred embroidery given by a foreman

to last. You must go up, some day, install your work there, imprint all that
has been promised in gold leaf. So, the little girl stops for a moment—and
naturally, at the bus stop she notices the sky-knife. She notices, so deeply,

perhaps in an a capella stance, with the hands placid at her sides. It is all
in the books: in Hamlet's tiny hands, in Medusa's sweet stone. The canner
by the steeple shimmers as it drops a diamond into the working line

and shivers, *who will find it?* It is a Mexican mystery; a black-shawled
locomotive leads there, the hair glows. La Llorona carries an anvil in her
womb, she has polished its phosphor point. Today is the Day of the Dead.

Say it again, in a wavy, accordion-like voice. I want to run in, to the rum-
colored train wheels, burrow into the rails, into their wayward ashes.
Go ahead—Mr. Emptiness, drink a cup of reddish, a sprig of ancient rime.

Put on your best tie. This is what I say, this is my incantation, my silly pants
of power leaping over a bridge. The deluge seeks me, he says, in a timbre and
timid presidential mask, American, you might say, global: Candy wrapper

skulls, sugary, Dalí-like crutches at the U.S.-trained Saudi barracks; how they
swing to the beat of a Miles Davis requiem—a trumpet slashes over missile
pumps, the ready blood. If my mother was here, if only she was here to rip

out the nails and Gala, descend for once and explode. And the little
commanders that snapped my uncle Geno's back: line them up—these green-
vested gendarmes with beige noses and shoot them—again, with the bluish seed

from the light. The grave only gives back the worthy (my grandmother said)—
a healer dressed as a baker, my father in a newspaper cap; maybe, a leg shadow
in a vine, falling from a Chamula cross at the Hill of the Saved and my sister,

Andrea, The Innocent, crushed at birth (her forehead's tender maps I followed). All
this—engraved on the ferns, bitten deep in a heart-shaped dishrag, a Klee Spider
after the grinning drills, the milling stones after the gasp.

Maga will dance a Tango with her favorite Buenos Aires rose, her hips sway
and her eyes burn through the veil and the men, enormous and hunched
over a round table, poker and chips, caught, dying. Yes, the dance will continue,

in its fragrant pomegranate string-bass beat
and all the hired hands, especially the hands
will rise.

Speckled w/ Razor

for Arturo Islas and Mama Chona, in memory

Open. Now—I say:
twist the bare knuckles. Speckled with razor
complexions, moons for lemon crates; tent flaps
in a stranger's backyard.

There is no pain. To learn from, to admonish? Perhaps,
a pin-up God, this knit-hoop of Holy Virgin draperies,
my velvet sister under tree shawls.

This is all, lion-tamer canopies—hushed,
battle cries frozen in the forearm. Oh,
the packer knows her cargo: tiny, human dolls,
a pheasant trenchcoat foreman; his looking-glass wife.

I live Uphill: a passcard. I carry.
Take the lorry. Listen—its carnival brain sings me,
radish tarps sway me, a makeshift sky lifts me.

LETTER
TO THE
HUNGRY
STUDENTS
OF BERLIN

Letter to the Hungry Students of Berlin

You
in the night
busy unlearning the world
from far far away . . .
                     Nelly Sachs

Big sky, above us.

Yes, above us,
above our flame-scented hair locks,
early and rebellious; the bluish dome casts down

—iciness,
unperturbed, without shadows.

The seduction of the asylum guard is attractive.
We've seen his military clinic, in rubble.
Nourishments,

behind the strings of the enamel cabinets.
Lines of *Asylanten* — refuge seekers

—tiny yellow stamped vials handled so
gently by the old Kommissars.

I smell licorice and turpentine.
Yes, today: this big sky,
tied close to our narrow chests.

We could almost say *the blue-green in the air.*

The blue-green in the air.

Orphaned alcohol spilled by strange gods.
Gifts from the unspeakable convex void.

The Goddess of Tempests and
New Brain Blood welcomes us.
I say this with caution and carelessness.
What is upon us?

What courses through our knock-knees?
Our bright hands of worker soap,
coffee and *Käsekuchen.*
Our rouged knuckles,
—steadfast now
in their reddish corduroy skin.

Look—we bear the flag of rouged knuckles. Yes,
we have a flag now, a skin flag.
Whose flag? Remember the Jewish-skin lamps?
They still burn, inside.

We are the skin lamps now,
at each subway station. In trampled asphalt fields,
wired clay, webbed neon leaves.

Listen
a tiny watery bulb-heart. Late
under the moon wind,
another autumn, it sings—ocean rage.

Who will touch our new faces, a green
branch held close to our shirts? A book of bread.
Ochre yeast on our lips, blushed with anise.

This bitter-sweet taste of cleanliness, I mean
the wild cleanliness after the avalanche.

Yes, the big sky.
Unfathomable. Our equation.
Who will decipher it?

Listen again:

Dark migrations.
Swiveled currents, disengaged rivers.
Curled fog, dark basso profundo,
in our name, yes, in our broken syllables
for sky
—a lifeboat sails with our voices.
Vigilant, spiritual.
Rising, settling.

What can I lift up
—rippled, enigmatic distances
blown-out daughters and sons?

Mothers, fathers; gone now,
to another age. Dug in, dug out in their humble straight
coats and dissident prayers.

My own mother, Lucia.
She would come out of her second-story
apartment in San Francisco, arm in arm
with my light-haired aunt, Teresa.
In the fifties. Together, go and drink

a cup of coffee—downtown canteens
where Mexican women were not allowed.

My mother
—walked where revolution gets tangled
in the skin and turns into a journey,

into the question of existence, vastness.

In the evening, in velvet solar heat,
we shall meet. On the same fallen granite.
I use that word *granite*.

Maybe in afternoon twilight, talk
in that typical fast manner of yours. You tell me
of the handsome gang onslaughts. Subway glass
smashed with Vietnamese blood. I tell you

of the migrant Mexicans, in the sorcery
called thirst. Inside train cars. Doubled up
behind the axle of an Oldsmobile—asking
for washer wax, asking for allowance,
straw for night soil. We'll talk

about your asylum hostels in Brandenburg,
Malchow, and Hoyerswerda. Doom's larvae.
Pesticide shacks prismatic, in Parlier, Visalia,
and Kingsburg, California.
A German restaurant there whispers:
What is the path of the Mexican ovens in the bakeries?

We play this music; listen to the horns.
In what forms? you say.
In the dance of chains and broken noses
—Störkraft, Noie Wert,
the KKK Junior League, Brutality Brittanika,

we all rock to the national beat
of Major Hurt.

Music?

My Americanness.
Your East-Westness.

"Metaphysical leprosy."
You laugh. An archaic term.

Xenophobia, you say.
My East-Westness, your Americanness.

We will despise this and then we'll stall.
Point to the human sidewalks; their blue thinness,
Gastarbeiter in their hunched worker overalls,
stagger down the avenues. On their migrant hands.

Mention Poland.
Never been there, none of us have.
Poland and Rózevicz (led to slaughter, at twenty-four, he

survived, yes).
We begin to speak of him here;
down the alley. Egg diners
on Saturday mornings, over toast,
hash browns, and juice.

Rózevicz and cigarettes,
Berlin and chocolates.

After we read his poems
we scribble a frenzy. On small wedge-tables.
Our musician friends lean over,
whisper into their lovers' ears,
their long hair over their eyes.

My musician friends use the term emptiness too.
They equate emptiness with fullness. They rejoiced when you
struck the Wall; the gray-speckled sex.
Sledgehammer music
across the mad seas.

My musician friends (students too)
—they play hard saxophones.
Rhythms of chalk dust,
spray cans; an old Mexican record
that resembles the smuggled Russian
Gypsy songs
—when Stalin was alive.

My pale, sallow-skinned
musician friends. Short coats or none at all
wander off.
We roam here. This is accurate,
yes, I think it is.
Video streams, bamboo.
A satellite system of delicate intimacies.

I know this much: Up there
—a giant mirror in the sky.
Mute flurries; in our own trueness.

In fashion malls underground. Without
the telescopic leash at times, Los Angeles
for example (the embers still burn).
We resolve ourselves.
Night nourishments, connecting to the wild,
we step,

to the possum detectives.
Scratch the pregnant bark, blare out its rap song.
Concentric. Halo-blood from tree stumps,
from their hearts. Next to the homeless one-eyeds.
Step to the local plazas, empty and shiny
after the rain. Cellophane,
stripped and naughty under our bare feet.
Presidential news stuck to our big toes.

Students of Berlin
are you hungry, as I am?
Are you hungrier, yes, you must be hungrier.

My wife, Maga, turns away from these discussions.
My wife. A seven-inch scar sewn across her belly.
An intruder wanted her. I search for him.
Day in day out.
I trace his knotted vernacular.
Every kiss slides down the rose thorns.

She reads Zagejewski.
She stares at Frida Kahlo. Flaring headlights
on the bedroom curtains.
She strokes her long black hair. It is black,
so black.

I fall into her arms. I yearn for comrades, I tell her.

But, you're an orphan, you
wouldn't know what brothers are. You
wouldn't know. She says, stroking her darkness.

We stop.
Gaze across the library, at an honorable bird
on the tightwire of the window ledge.
The bird is minuscule,
a blue jack, wet and steady.
Little cosmic engines on silvery animal tracks,
sniffing out our lives behind the glass.
Measuring us for rain, for bread.

Big sky, up—it is frayed, riddled
in blood-bath gardenias.

It is a falling sky. Falling to its own grave,
but where is the grave for skies? In Bosnia they know
about the sky grave. In Los Angeles (the embers).
There are blasts everywhere. I'd like to say
that this awakens us.

As I speak I want
to slither out of my mouth cavity.

I want to write of love
in the face of disaster.

When I eat
my favorite powdered sweet cakes,
the reptile pokes me in the ribs,
a sexual deepness in its eyes;
large crimson, loose.

But, then I slump through the short
arduous light of the theaters, the palisades.
I'd like to say I am walking with a little girl
still in my irises. Who do you walk with?

Yes, who do you walk with? Who
still resides in your eyes?

Do you follow her songs?
Into the tilted factories, the smeared taxis,

the stunted universities, into the parlor of bank notes,
in the cramped cook house where the dark-skinned
humans still stoop and pitch the daily lettuce bags,
the daily radish box,

our daily buckets of fruit meats? A half-cup of red sausage? Is it so?

I fall back,
I sleep more than I should, I lie down by the wrinkled sidewalk, draw chalk circles;

meet the hunger artists.
You know them.
They paint their cheeks with crazy eights.
Their sex is full grown, sprawled open.

Their enlarged livers
push out of the thorax, they push out
in a modern shape, the Autobahn, for example.
They speak of fluorescence,
a colossal fixture. Raised hands and necks;
artificial light, over our dark stores,
weary with revolutionary ambitions.

Maybe we'll slip into your new century,
—under your new country—
fondle its embossed fuses.
Tree rot and sperm,
breast milk, tears, spit, and cement fodder,
bullet-sized droppings from above.

We gravitate toward you, the spirit here, inside gravitates.
Well-pressed university shirts; anarchic spiders with bow ties
and briefcases. We weave
an unparalleled labyrinth.

We slide downwards, into the Southern streets.
Barefoot, we arch and kiss,
we exchange notes on the soft ends of the earth,
on the military parade; eerie screens.
Velcro jackets pulling skin
off and on, off and on.

We listen with excited ears, mechanical and fantastic
—with a jealous lover's heat. Our blue greenness speaks in
low scales.

We lean to the cloud and water music;
all night fancies, when clouds lie over clouds
and shape deep thighs over our houses.
These are our charms. The maps we follow.
This is how our brown face is cultured, in this scale, full of
sky shapes, ancient, blistering, alone
with each other. Old light
and new light.

Glossary

Abarrotes	Groceries
Arroz con leche	Chicano and Mexican dessert: sweet rice pudding
Artistas	Artists
Asylanten	Asylum seekers in Germany
Aztlán	The mythological and historical point of origin of the Aztecs, now the U.S. Southwest
Baglame	Turkish stringed instrument
Banderilla	Short barbed lance used in bullfights
Bolas	Dollars
Brujería	Act of healing (usually a negative term)
Cabrón	Stupid, fool
Café con leche	Coffee mixed with steaming hot milk
Calavera	Skull
Calcos	Working-class term for shoes
Caldo de res	Beef and vegetable soup
Calle	Street
Camaradas	Comrades, friends
Camisas	Shirts

Canas	Gray hair
Cante jondo	Andalusian "deep song," magical consciousness
Caoba	Mahogany
Carnal	Brother, close friend
Cartón	Money, cardboard
Casa	House
Cena	Dinner
Central, La	Main train station in Mexico City
Chicana, Chicano	If you can't guess this, try again
Chicos con carne de res	Dried corn kernels mixed with beef and bean stew
Chilacayote	Wild pear
Chile huero	Yellow wax pepper
Chile piquín	Small red pepper, native to the Southwest
Chiles colorados	Dried New Mexican red peppers
Chistes	Jokes
Clika	Clique, group of persons
Clínica	Clinic
Colonia	Neighborhood, district
Comunidad	Community
Copal	Mexican Indian incense
Coquitos	Mexican coconut candy
Cuadrado	Big and strong
Cuentista	Storyteller
Cuentos	Stories
Curandero	Working-class religious healer
Danza	An Aztec religious dance
Danzante	A member of the Aztec Danza group
Delicados	Brand of Mexican working-class cigarettes
Día de los muertos	Day of the Dead, a Mexican religious holiday to honor the dead, celebrated November 2
Enjarradora	Hearth maker
Están bien locos	They are crazy in a big way
Estufa	Stove
Familia	Family
Federales	Feds, cops

Feria	Money, fair
Firme carruchas	Cool cars
Flor de calabaza	Squash flower used in Chicano and Mexican cuisine
Frijoles colorados con salsa	Mexican dish consisting of red beans, beef, and hot sauce
Gastarbeiter	Migrant workers in Germany
Gente	People
Greña	Hair
Grifa	Marihuana
Güiro	An Afro-Cuban percussion instrument
Guitarras	Guitars
Hamón	From *jamón,* ham
Hipódromo	Racetrack
Huaraches	Indian sandals made of leather and rubber
Huipil	Indian woman's garment
Incensario	Incense holder
Ipal Nemowani	From Ipal Nemohuani, the Aztec deity of the Far and Near
Jale	Job, work
Käsekuchen	German pastry
Kawela	From *cajuela,* car trunk
La del sol	Referring to the Sun Dance
La hacemos	We can do it; we'll survive
Lana	Money, wool
Leña	Firewood
Let's gotas	Let's go
Libros	Books
Licuados	Vegetable and fruit drinks mixed in a blender
Llanta	Tire
Llorona, la	Ghost-woman who appears in Mexican and Chicano folk literature
Lomo	Beef
Longo	Long Beach

Maestro	Honorific term for the leader of the Aztec Danza, a Nahuatl religious ceremonial dance community known as the Danzantes de la Conquista
Manta	Muslin, blanket
Me voy a casar en los estados	I am going to get married in the States
Mecánico	Mechanic
Merengue	Afro-Cuban upbeat dance
Migrante	Migrant farm worker
Milagros	Miracles
Milpa	Cornfield
Mojo	African-American amulet
Mole	Mexican sauce made of various ingredients, including chiles, nuts, raisins, herbs and spices, and chocolate
Movida	An "angle," a "move"
Movimiento	Chicano socio-political movement for social justice
Nietas, Nietos	Granddaughters, grandsons
Noie Wert	German skinhead band
Novia	Girlfriend
Orale	An expression of agreement: all right, right on, excellent
Orejas	Ears
Otro, el	The other
Pachucos	Chicano working-class rebel youth, with a distinct style and language emerging from the East Los Angeles "zoot suit" riots in the forties
Parisa	Contemporary Middle Eastern singer
Pata de mula	Black clams in their juice
Penacho	Feathered Aztec warrior breast cloth used in religious dances
Peyote	Hallucinogenic cactus native to central Mexico
Piola	Money, string
Planchados	Ironed, pressed
Porche	Front porch

Pulque	Working-class liquor made from the fermented juice of the agave
Pura piña	Pure pineapple
Raza	The people, Chicano nation
Refín	Food, chow
Rifa	Prize, lottery
Ropa	Clothes
Rugola	Jewish sweet cakes
Ruta maya	New road leading from Ocosingo, Chiapas, into the Mayan lowlands
Sanwishes	From sandwiches
Somos mazatecas	We are Mazatec Indians
Sopaipillas	New Mexican deep-fried turnovers
Störkraft	German skinhead band
Tambores	Drums
Tarahumaras	Indian tribe in the Mexican Northwest
Teatristas	Chicano Theater participants, in the Movimiento Chicano
Teatro de los Niños	Chicano children's theater of the seventies
Tevoyacurar	"Imagoingtocureyou"
Tiendita	Sundry goods store
Tierra mojada	Wet earth
Tin Tan	Mexican comedian and film celebrity of the fifties known for his zoot suit attire and use of Chicano working-class speech
Tina	Large tin wash bucket
Tortas	Mexican and Chicano sandwiches made with bread rolls
Tortillas de harina	Flour tortillas
Tripas	Cooked beef tripe
Turista	Tourist
Varrio	From *barrio,* neighborhood
Vato	Dude
Vecinos	Neighbors

Viejitas	Old women
Viejito	Old man
Visitas	Visits
Volío	From *bolillo,* bread roll
Zócalo	Church plaza in Mexico City

About the Author

JUAN FELIPE HERRERA was born in 1948 in Fowler, California. Since the mid-1960s he has been active as a poet, editor, *teatrista,* and teacher in various universities and California communities. He holds an M.F.A. in poetry from the University of Iowa Writers' Workshop and an M.A. in social anthropology from Stanford.

Herrera has published four books of poetry (*Rebozos of Love, Exiles of Desire, Facegames,* and *Akrílica*), and his work has appeared in numerous literary journals. His most recent awards include the Lila Wallace National Reading Tour Fellowship (1992) and the University of Iowa Literary Journal Award for Poetry (1990). Presently he is an associate professor of Chicano and Latin American Studies at California State University in Fresno. He lives with the poet, Margarita Luna Robles, and children, Robert and Marlene.